"Glory be, here are recipes for second-to-none cookies, cakes, bread, biscuits, jams and jellies, even Aunt Darla's Smoky Pimento Cheese and Brian's legendary granola. For bakers, eaters, and hungry adventurers, the Holy Grail has arrived."

—MICHAEL STERN,
COAUTHOR OF *ROADFOOD*

....

"I have known few people with greater passion for what they do than Brian Noyes. It shows in *every* crumb of everything he cooks and in every word in this magnificent and stunningly beautiful book."

—JOHN CURRENCE,
CHEF AND AUTHOR OF
BIG BAD BREAKFAST

....

"The creation of a dream, the accidental serendipity, the making of a family at the Red Truck Bakery, the hard work, and the eventual realization of this community bedrock is literally baked into every page."

—ANDREW ZIMMERN,
TRAVELER, CHEF, WRITER,
AND TEACHER

"Brian Noyes is a master of subtle subversion who slips pawpaws in chess pie, crumbles pretzels in pie crust, and bakes an almond cake that conjures up those delicious Chinese takeout cookies with the almond divots. His *Red Truck Bakery Cookbook* redefines American baking in the most inclusive and progressive ways."

—JOHN T. EDGE,
DIRECTOR, SOUTHERN
FOODWAYS ALLIANCE

....

"Pldse xcuse mu stcky fngers but I can't stop eating Red Truck's glorious granola long enough to write! This great little cookbook is a treasure. It holds a story of passion and persistence. It is a song of love to a region and its people. And it's chock-full of recipes to make you and those you love dance around the kitchen in anticipation."

—RONNI LUNDY,
AUTHOR OF *VICTUALS*

Red Truck
BAKERY
COOKBOOK

Gold-Standard Recipes from America's
Favorite Rural Bakery

Brian Noyes

PHOTOGRAPHS BY
Andrew Thomas Lee

CLARKSON POTTER/PUBLISHERS
NEW YORK

For Dwight, and in memory of my uncle Stan

Contents

My Red Truck Road Trip

John Wayne made me a tuna sandwich.

I was the nineteen-year-old art director of a weekly newspaper in Corona del Mar, California, and had an appointment with the actor's housekeeper to return a heavy carton of framed photographs we had borrowed for a feature profile. Nearly dropping the box, I kicked the door several times with my foot as a way of knocking (hey, I was a teenager). John Wayne himself was suddenly in my face, scowling. I handed him the box of pictures, apologized, and he invited me in.

"Ya wanna tuna sandwich?" he asked.

I had just eaten but I wasn't going to pass *that* up. He led me through his house on Newport Bay and we ended up in the kitchen overlooking his yacht, the *Wild Goose*. I watched the process closely as he toasted hearty slices of wheat bread, spreading each with mayonnaise. He made the tuna salad with a good pinch of salt to boost the flavor, adding more mayo, chopped sweet pickles, and celery. He then plopped a big mound onto a pile of lettuce. Before adding the top slice of toast, he looked right at me and smashed a fistful of potato chips into the tuna filling, commanding in his drawl, "This is why you'll like this."

I've made tuna sandwiches the same way ever since. John Wayne's lesson sticks with me forty years later: there are no rules.

• • •

My mom wasn't an adventurous cook but, with a family of seven to feed, she and my newspaperman dad fed us in as economical a manner as possible (pancakes for dinner seemed like a genuine treat). Bargain margarine was a staple in our fridge, and it wasn't until I was working myself that I tasted real butter for the first time. A coworker brought in homemade banana bread and I told her it was the best thing I had ever eaten. She glowed—until she realized I was referring to the pat of butter on top of my slice. My culinary appreciation was, well, lacking.

My uncle Stan took me under his wing and set me on the path of baking. He loved to tinker in his Florida kitchen and would ship his latest breads to me in California. I took that as a challenge and reciprocated, proudly sending my own baked goods across the country. A Florida-postmarked carton would arrive a couple of weeks later with *his* versions of my recipes. He would mark up the original I had sent with a red pen indicating corrections he thought were needed to make the items tastier.

Whenever I flew to the Sunshine State to visit my cousins, I'd saddle up next to my uncle in his Clearwater kitchen to work with him on his latest baking project. After a spirited back-and-forth over the better part of a year, we nailed a multigrain wheat bread full of golden raisins, dried cranberries, and walnuts. (Spoiler alert: you can find it on page 160.)

• • •

Early on my career path, I stayed with publishing, not bread baking or tuna sandwich making, because I caught the bug from my dad, who used to let me drop by his newspaper office after school. As he said, once you get printer's ink in your blood, it's there forever. I moved to the nation's capital in 1984 when legendary editor Ben Bradlee hired me as the art director of the *Washington Post*'s new Sunday magazine. In addition to my daily editorial routine, I worked alongside revered *Post* food critic Phyllis Richman and her assistant, Tom Sietsema, packaging their weekly restaurant columns and annual dining guides.

My pal (and now spouse) Dwight McNeill joined me on weekly photography visits as we scouted the restaurants they were writing about. Over time, the *Post*'s special dining issues became my favorite projects to design.

As Dwight and I took trips throughout the southern United States, we searched out funky cafés, barbecue joints, groceries, and bakeries. For our compass, we kept a copy of Jane and Michael Stern's *Roadfood* in the glove box. I didn't know it then, but that guidebook helped inspire me to think about ditching a life in publishing and opening a charming little food joint.

My publishing career took me from the *Washington Post* to art directorships at *House & Garden*, *Preservation*, *Architecture*, and *Smithsonian* magazines; later I rejoined the *Washington Post*, which I'd sorely missed. I wasn't getting any younger, though, and I figured that if I were ever going to follow my passion to launch a food business, I'd better get on board soon. I burned up my vacation hours as I immersed myself in a professional baking and cooking education. I enrolled in the Culinary Institute of America (the other CIA) in New York, training in café breads and pastries, and volunteered for the three a.m. bake for the school's restaurants. I followed Chicago restaurateur Rick Bayless to the CIA's program in Oaxaca, Mexico, where we cooked regional cuisine in a former convent. I even spent a week taking bread classes at King Arthur Flour's headquarters in Norwich, Vermont. I learned much more at the prestigious L'Academie de Cuisine, a baking and cooking school just outside of Washington, DC, in classes led by Mark Ramsdell, former assistant to White House pastry chef Roland Mesnier.

• • •

In 1997, Dwight and I moved from the top floor apartment of a DC row house to our own home in

Arlington County, Virginia, across the Potomac. I had grown tomatoes and peppers on our urban balcony, and was excited that our new house had a yard where I could plant a proper garden. Even though we could see the Washington Monument from our neighborhood, Arlington felt less like a city and more country-like, with a local farmer's market—and a county fair.

Just as peaches were coming into season, I decided to enter some jam into competition at the Arlington County Fair. Mary Jones, an old friend of ours, had stopped by with a tub of crystallized ginger. I chopped a handful of her ginger; added a little cinnamon, nutmeg, and sugar to the sliced peaches; ladled my boiling jam into sterilized jars; and sealed them up. The results tasted delicious to me—sweet, well-spiced and a little zingy from the ginger—but one never knows how judges will react. I dropped off my entry, crossed my fingers, and headed to the airport for a long-planned visit to California.

Dwight called me a day later with the competition results. "Sit down for this," he said. "You got an honorable mention."

I yawned. "Great. A ribbon for the kitchen."

Then he added, "You also won the theme award. And, well, first place. And, by the way, you were named Grand Champion." The judges told him it was the crystallized ginger that swayed them. I wrote a story for the *Post*'s food section about my big inaugural win. After the taste of victory, there was no turning back.

• • •

A few years later, we bought a weekend getaway: a small farmhouse on a few acres in the village of Orlean, the heart of Virginia's Piedmont hunt country one hour west of DC. I planted an orchard of peach, apple, sour cherry, and persimmon trees. Always thinking like an art director, I thought we needed an old truck on the farm, and bought a bright red 1954 Ford F-100 I found online. The seller turned out to be fashion designer Tommy Hilfiger; he'd used the restored

truck on his Connecticut farm and had it shipped to me in Virginia.

I began baking breads, pies, and granola on Friday nights out at the farmhouse. The next morning, I would hop into the old red truck and deliver my goods to three rural stores: the Village Green in Orlean, Epicurious Cow in Amissville, and R.H. Ballard in Little Washington. The baking was a hit. People started showing up half an hour before the stores opened, waiting for me to pull up with the truck's bed full of still-warm goodies, inspiring me to dub my fledgling business the Red Truck Bakery. I designed a crude website and offered up my more-durable baked goods for shipping anywhere in the country. How hard could it be?

Through a crazy twist of fate, *New York Times* food writer Marian Burros enjoyed my fruit pies, quiche, and granola at a picnic in nearby Rappahannock County. The Red Truck Bakery led the *Times* story of Marian's fifteen favorite national food purveyors in her 2007 Christmas roundup. My website went from twenty-four hits one day to 57,000 the next. Dwight took time off from work to help me pack up homemade baked goods, and the mailman scratched his head when he pulled into our driveway and saw the huge load that was waiting to head out with him.

It was time to open a real bakery. So in 2008, I left publishing behind and began my new life as a baker.

• • •

I began looking for a space in Virginia's rural Rappahannock and Fauquier counties, but nothing was large enough or felt right. Broadening my search, I stumbled across a rundown 1921 Esso filling station in the Fauquier county seat of Warrenton, Virginia, twenty minutes south of Marshall. It was perched on a corner in the tree-lined center of town, across the road from the library and next to the historic courthouse and county buildings. When I drove down the street, it felt like I had been transported into a Norman Rockwell painting. It was perfect.

I signed a five-year lease on that old service station and worked for months to get the look of the bakery just right. Dwight, a residential architect, came up with our rural-yet-sophisticated mercantile look, with old schoolhouse lighting and lots of bead-board paneling. Every detail was important and none was too small. Once an art director, always an art director! I bought new and used mixers, refrigerators, three mammoth ovens, and buckets of baking tools. A neighbor peeked at the progress and told me it looked like something right out of Napa Valley.

• • •

And then the Great Recession hit and the economy blew up. My investors suddenly had cold feet; I was all alone, but at that point I was all in—I had cashed out my savings to make the Red Truck Bakery happen. I knew it would work—I wouldn't have taken the plunge if I was unsure about it—but Dwight was wildly nervous.

I closely followed the incoming Obama administration's efforts to improve the economic problems they'd inherited, and I put my faith—and future—in the president's plans. With hard work and eighteen-hour days, I hired four part-time employees and we opened the bakery on July 31, 2009. I kept the bakery afloat with a small short-term loan from an acquaintance, although I stayed awake many nights worrying about paying suppliers and making payroll.

It took several years until the economy improved, and I'm glad we hung on. We rebounded, and word was out about what we were doing in our small town. *Esquire*, *Southern Living*, *Garden & Gun*, *Saveur*, and other publications wrote about us. I was caught off guard, however, the day I looked up and saw Michael Stern of Roadfood.com walk in the store. He and Jane Stern were my first food heroes, thanks to that beat-up copy of *Roadfood* Dwight and I had used for years on car trips. The Sterns have become our loudest and proudest fans, shouting our praises all over the country.

While baking in the Warrenton kitchen, I was close enough to my computer to hear a "ding" every time an emailed shipping order arrived. One morning I heard a ding, then a ding-ding, then a ding-ding-ding-ding-ding, and I logged in to see what the fuss was about. In just fifteen minutes we had received eighty orders for our granola, and they were all from Wisconsin or Minnesota. Google led me to that morning's *Milwaukee Journal-Sentinel* story about the Travel Channel's Andrew Zimmern. In the middle of the interview, a reporter pointed out that Zimmern was known for eating bizarre foods and asked what he eats at home. His answer: "For breakfast, I eat Greek yogurt and Red Truck Bakery Granola—the best granola in North America." That's all it took.

The bakery had become a crazy success. Oprah Winfrey found out about us and her *O Magazine* named us one of their favorite online food sites. *Bon Appétit* editor Adam Rapoport named our Double-Chocolate Moonshine Cake (page 135) one of 2015's top food picks—on NBC's *Today* show four days before Christmas, and nearly crashed our website with hundreds of last-minute orders we weren't prepared for. We've been named one of "America's Best Small-Town Bakeries" by *Travel+Leisure*, and *Garden & Gun* judge Sean Brock gave "Made in the South" honors to our Sweet Potato Pecan Pie (The Presidential Pie) (page 71). Customers driving up the East Coast arrive with a copy of our story from *Southern Living* under their arm and tell us they drove two hours out of their way to visit us.

Much of what we make can be shipped nationwide through our website, and I'm always amazed that people in far-off states find out about us and seek us out. It's unfathomable that a family in Boston or Seattle or Santa Fe is serving *our* dessert at *their* holiday dinner.

• • •

With the cheers came more business, and we quickly outgrew our little gas station bakery. In 2013, we stopped taking Christmas shipping orders the first week of December, way too early in the season, since we were overwhelmed with hundreds of orders awaiting baking and packing for UPS. To get us through the month, our landlord offered up empty office space down the street to act as a shipping center. But pushing carts of freshly baked cakes down a sidewalk in freezing rain, ice, and snow had the potential for disaster, and we needed to find a permanent solution.

County supervisor Peter Schwartz stopped in to help and encouraged me to consider the village of Marshall, where a family-owned fifty-year-old grocery store had just closed. Plenty of vacant buildings were available, and I fell in love with two adjoining historic mercantile buildings on Main Street, across from the post office. Peter gathered investors and helped put our finances in order, and Dwight reenlisted as my architect. We gutted the two buildings, ignoring their previous incarnations as an ashtray bar and restaurant (one wall was lined with off-track betting machines!), and instead took the buildings back to look a bit like they must have when they opened as a pharmacy, Masonic lodge, and sweet shop in the early 1910s.

• • •

On Labor Day in 2015, we opened our new headquarters. Robert Duvall, one of our first customers, cut the ribbon for us—actually, the Western actor preferred to use a coil of farm rope and a pocketknife to saw through it. Our friend Franny Thomas helped curate a Red Truck soundtrack of rootsy ramblers, including Jason Isbell, The Lone Bellow, and Hazel Dickens, putting a twang in the bakery air. We had a sign installed on the local interstate—one of those "Food Next Exit" postings with our logo—and it brings in an amazing number of families pulling off for a rest stop, and leaving with pies and bags of bread.

I like to think we helped spark a renaissance in sleepy Marshall. In addition to a unique rural bakery, Main Street now has a butcher shop manned by a tattooed hipster staff, a new organic market and café—and our good friends Neal and Star Wavra have opened an award-winning farm-to-table restaurant, Field & Main, directly across the street from us.

It wouldn't have been possible without our talented staffers who joined us through the years, our unflinching group of investors, and especially the enthusiastic customers who make it all worthwhile. They ask to use our stores for election victory parties, wedding brunches, fashion shoots, book signings, school tours, summer camp baking classes, and even a TV commercial. Customers want the old red truck at their weddings with a pie bar served out of the back, or with a tailgate spread for the Virginia Gold Cup steeplechase races. Robert Duvall settles in for a tuna sandwich with James Caan (I got to tell them both my John Wayne story) and chats up the local kids enjoying brownies. Singer Mary Chapin Carpenter pulls out her laptop at a window seat near the kitchen to work on her new album, keeping an eye on her dogs outside.

As his last year in office wound down, I sent a note to President Obama explaining how things turned out for us after I stuck with his administration's retooling of the economy. A month later his chief speechwriter, Cody Keenan, hand-delivered a letter from Obama; we sent him off with a sweet-potato pecan pie for the president. That led to an Obama salute, on his Facebook page and the White House website, to our story and success on Pi Day (3.14—March 14, 2016).

• • •

I never imagined that my little food idea, born while daydreaming at a newspaper job, would grow into two locations with nearly fifty employees, shipping thousands of items each year across the country. It's come full circle: I talked Red Rooster Coffee in Floyd, Virginia, into blending a bold, robust "Bulldog Edition" coffee for us, whose name and packaging honor my former *Washington Post* editor, Ben Bradlee, and the early morning edition of the paper. As my dad promised, there's still printer's ink in my blood.

THE

LARDER

There are ingredients you will see in this cookbook over and over again. Some of them are the basics of baking, while others are specialty products that are called for only on occasion. In the case of the former, these are good things to have on hand. In the case of the latter, it's especially worth going through the trouble to track them down, because you'll be able to taste the results. Where applicable, though, I offer up another suggestion that is available at the average grocery store. I also indicate when it's okay to use store-bought ingredients as a substitute for the suggested subrecipes.

White Lily All-Purpose Flour
For 130 years, this has been the gold standard for Southern biscuits. If you can't find it in your local grocery store, it's readily available online, though any all-purpose flour will suffice. If you choose to use self-rising flour, you should eliminate the baking soda and baking powder from the recipes and add an extra 2 tablespoons self-rising flour to the given measurement instead.

Butter
We always use unsalted butter; it tastes cleaner and lets us control the amount of salt in a recipe. We found that European-style butter, such as Plugrá, works best, although a good American unsalted butter, such as Land O'Lakes or Breakstone, also works well.

Buttermilk
I find that full-fat buttermilk works best in baking; it gives better texture and taste than the fat-free (or low-fat) version. Use whatever version you can find.

Eggs
Always large, preferably local and organic, and definitely cage-free.

Salt
Readily available, kosher salt is a foundational ingredient for any baker worth his or her…well, you know. If a recipe calls for sea salt as a finishing touch, I'm a big fan of J.Q. Dickinson's salt from West Virginia.

Baking Soda and Baking Powder
You should have both on hand, stored in airtight containers. Make sure to replace them one year after opening or after the use-by date, whichever comes first, to ensure they are at peak strength.

Active Dry Yeast
There are several styles of yeast available, but our recipes are designed to work with this type. Store it in an airtight container in your freezer, where it will stay fresh for a year.

Pure Vanilla Extract
Please avoid using imitation vanilla extract, as it will impart a chemical flavor and create an inferior product; it's not worth the savings. We prefer Nielsen-Massey's Madagascar bourbon pure vanilla extract.

Dark Brown Sugar
Occasionally, a recipe will call for light brown sugar; otherwise, use dark. Always pack brown sugar when measuring it.

Granulated Sugar
There's no need to spend anything more than you have to on this ingredient. Your grocery store's in-house brand is fine.

Dried Spices
Though many people open a bottle or tin and leave it on their rack till it's done, it's worth replacing spices after six months. The fresher the spices, the more intense their flavors. I recommend always having the following spices on hand: ground cinnamon, ground allspice, ground ginger, ground or whole nutmeg, ground cloves, smoked paprika, red pepper flakes, and dried sage. Please use only fresh rosemary, not the dry version.

Meyer Lemons
There's an intensity and complexity to this varietal that trounces all others. Deep yellow or even orange colored, they lack the mouth-puckering acidity of most other lemons. Instead, they possess an added sweetness and a perfumed orange-like zest that's unlike anything else in the citrus section. Meyer lemons are available from November through May in larger grocery stores, or can be purchased online at whiteflowerfarm.com. Regular lemons can be substituted, but you'll miss the nuances of Meyer lemons.

Sorghum Syrup
A fair number of our recipes are sweetened with this Southern syrup, which is made from the juices pressed from the stalks of tall green sorghum plants (not from corn, as many people think). Lighter and less intense than molasses (though you may sometimes see it sold as sorghum molasses), and smoother and more buttery than maple syrup, sorghum has a unique golden flavor. Substituting either molasses or maple syrup may not always yield the intended results, so I've indicated when you can make a substitution. If you don't live in the South, you can purchase sorghum syrup from a number of online retailers.

THE

TOOLSHED

Most of the recipes in this cookbook can be easily made using gear available in the average kitchen. However, there are times when specialty equipment will make a noticeable difference. Unless indicated otherwise, you can find these items at most any kitchen store or online; we use webrestaurant.com, williams-sonoma.com, and surlatable.com.

Stand Mixer

This will be your workhorse, helping you prep cookies, cakes, breads, and frostings faster than if you did it by hand. Make sure you have paddle, whisk, and dough hook attachments to handle a variety of tasks.

Handheld Electric Mixer

Though this is not a necessity, handheld mixers can be incredibly helpful in cutting down the prep time and saving your arms a workout. I'm especially fond of mine at home during the holiday season when I'm baking up endless batches of cookies. A hand mixer is usable as a substitute for a stand mixer in most cases, but you'll need a more powerful and stable stand mixer when beating or kneading heavier doughs.

Food Processor

This is invaluable when you need to finely chop up ingredients or blend multiple ingredients together. I like the ones with larger capacity, ranging from 11 cups to 16 cups, but the recipes in this book will work with a standard 8-cup model. I still prefer a knife for chopping herbs.

Pastry Blender/Pastry Cutter

When you're cutting chilled butter into a flour mixture, this handheld tool with narrow metal strips or wires allows you to break it down into pea-sized pieces quickly and efficiently.

Biscuit Cutter

A circular 3-inch cookie cutter will do the trick nicely.

Offset Spatula

When it comes time to frost cakes, this is an invaluable tool for smoothing sides, leveling tops, and ensuring they look as gorgeous as they taste.

Wire Whisk

A medium whisk works best; if it's too big, it will be unwieldy.

Serrated Knife

Get one with a 10-inch blade to cut breads. I use mine for nearly everything.

Rimmed Baking Sheets

A couple of 13 x 18-inch baking sheets, along with raised wire racks that fit into them, are invaluable for a variety of tasks.

Bundt Pans

When a recipe calls for one, go with a 10-inch, 12-cup fluted Bundt pan. Straightforward, simple designs are fine, but more ornate molds add a little splash for special occasions.

Rotating Cake Stand

This will make frosting your cakes much easier; plus, it's a great way to showcase your creation at the center of the table or on your kitchen counter.

Wire-Mesh Strainers

We keep several sizes on hand with various sizes of mesh. We suggest using these for sifting your flour and confectioners' sugar before each use. I think medium-mesh strainers work best—you don't need to purchase a flour sifter.

Canning Pot with Jar Rack

You only need these items if you plan on preserving any of the jams, jellies, or pickles in this cookbook. Find them in the canning section of your local hardware store, the canning aisle of some grocery stores, or online.

SOME QUICK KITCHEN ADVICE

You have all the equipment you need and your larder is stocked with the basics, so you're almost ready to bake. However, you should first read through these tips and tricks. They will save you time and help ensure your baked goods turn out phenomenally, so those lucky enough to enjoy them will compliment you endlessly and ask you to share your recipes. (Tell 'em to buy a copy of the book!)

Mise en Place

The first thing I learned at the Culinary Institute of America and L'Academie de Cuisine is the practice of *mise en place* (French for "put in place")—it's the routine of having every ingredient measured out, sliced, peeled, and grated before you start your baking or cooking. There's a reason instructors and professional chefs start with this and why I insist that my staff do this—having everything ready before you begin eliminates any head scratching later as you wonder if you've already added baking powder, or you discover that you don't have any fresh thyme or buttermilk on hand. It's an organizational habit that is imperative to success. Read through a recipe first and prep all the ingredients and grab all the pans, bowls, and tools you'll need. It really helps.

Measuring Out or Mixing Sticky Substances

If you're working with sorghum syrup, honey, molasses, maple syrup, or anything else that tends to cause a sticky mess, first coat your utensils with a nonstick cooking spray. This will ensure these syrups easily slide out of measuring cups, measuring spoons, and bowls.

Citrus Zest and Sugar

You'll discover that if a recipe calls for sugar mixed with grated lemon zest, orange zest, or fresh ginger, I mention it early for a good reason. After grating the zest into the sugar, a few minutes of sitting allows the sugar to become highly infused with the flavor. It also prevents the pores of the peel from closing up so the zest continues to add fragrance: you get more bang for your buck.

Adding Flour to a Batter

You'll see in our cake recipes that we add flour a third at a time when blending the batter, alternating with a liquid and blending again. It prevents the heavier ingredients from weighing down any light fluffing you've already done, and keeps everything mixed evenly. Typically you'll start with the flour and other dry ingredients (other than sugar): add one-third of the total amount of flour needed, mix, then add half the total amount of milk or other liquid and mix again. Repeat with half the remaining flour, mix, add the remaining milk, mix, then add the remaining flour and give it a final mix.

Working the Dough

When bread doughs require kneading to develop gluten, kneading by hand can provide an immense amount of satisfaction; you can really feel the dough—the texture, the softness, and the elasticity. Conversely, biscuit doughs require a light touch so they don't become tough—handle those doughs as little as possible. When making biscuits, using cold butter keeps it from mashing too much into the flour; the cold bits of butter add rise and texture.

Breakfast Fixins

Rise and Shine Biscuits

Makes 16 to 20 biscuits

This simple staple is the foundation of Southern baking, and every chef has his or her own recipe. Mine is based on my grandmother's, though I've added some newer techniques gleaned over the years from several regions of the South. Justise Robbins of Chef & the Farmer restaurant in Kinston, North Carolina, may well make the gold standard of biscuits, and I also learned what to do—and what *not* to do—at the International Biscuit Festival in Knoxville. Our pal Carrie Morey at Callie's Charleston Biscuits in South Carolina taught me to push the biscuits tightly together on a baking sheet or cast-iron skillet so that they rise up with one another to soaring heights.

Don't use an electric mixer for these. It's all about a light touch, so grab a large bowl, a pastry cutter if you have one (or two butter knives if you don't), and flour your clean hands. The dough will be wetter than you expect; please don't add more flour thinking it will help—it won't. Trust us. You'll need to chill the unbaked biscuits in the refrigerator for an hour before baking.

5¼ cups unbleached all-purpose flour, sifted, plus more for dusting

1 tablespoon baking powder

1¼ teaspoons baking soda

1 tablespoon plus 3 teaspoons kosher salt

2 tablespoons sugar

1 cup (2 sticks) unsalted butter, chilled and cubed, plus 4 tablespoons (½ stick), melted

½ cup heavy cream

3 cups buttermilk

1. In a large bowl, whisk together the flour, baking powder, baking soda, 1 tablespoon plus 2 teaspoons of the salt, and the sugar. Cut the chilled cubed butter into the flour mixture with your fingers, two knives, or a pastry cutter (do not use a mixer) until broken down into pea-sized pieces. Combine the heavy cream with the buttermilk in a measuring cup and add it to the dry mixture all at once. Using a spatula or a plastic scraper, fold in the buttermilk as quickly and as gently as possible. Flour your hands and reach into the bowl and under the dough, flipping it around. Mix it up without being too tough on the dough. The dough will be very wet, but manageable.

2. Turn the dough out onto a lightly floured surface and, working lightly, use your hands to pat it into a roughly 9 x 12-inch rectangle about 1 inch tall. Lightly sprinkle flour across the top of the dough and pat it with your hands until the flour has been absorbed (if you leave it atop the dough, your biscuits will have unwelcome flour pockets).

(recipe continues)

RED TRUCK BAKERY COOKBOOK

3. Flour the bottom of the dough and your work surface. With a scraper, fold the dough in half lengthwise, and repeat flouring it and patting it out with your hands. Repeat the process a total of four times. The dough will still be wet, but much more manageable. Don't add more flour, but again pat the dough into a roughly 9 x 12-inch rectangle about 1 inch tall.

4. Dip a 3-inch biscuit cutter into flour and cut as many biscuits as you can from the dough, pressing straight down with the cutter each time (don't twist the cutter or the biscuits won't rise as well). Reroll the scraps as needed. Using a baking sheet lined with parchment paper, or a cast-iron skillet, place the biscuits so they are touching one another. Refrigerate the biscuit dough for at least 1 hour and up to 3 hours.

5. Preheat the oven to 400°F. Line a portion of your workspace with newspaper and set a raised wire rack on top.

6. Remove the biscuits from the refrigerator and bake for 14 minutes, turning the pan halfway through, until the tops are a light golden brown.

7. Meanwhile, in a small bowl, mix the 4 tablespoons melted butter with the remaining 1 teaspoon salt.

8. Immediately transfer the biscuits to the wire rack and brush their tops with the salted melted butter. Serve warm slathered with butter and/or preserves.

9. The biscuits will keep in a tightly sealed plastic bag at room temperature for up to a day, or in the freezer for up to six months.

Blueberry and Ginger Scones

Makes 18 scones

When the mercury spikes in mid-July, customers love munching on these summery scones for breakfast or as a midafternoon pick-me-up. Though we do make these during blueberry season, I've found that dried blueberries yield the best results. I searched all over for the best ones to use for this recipe and in our Red Truck Bakery Granola (page 32), calling in samples from purveyors all over the country. We must have tried a couple dozen options.

On a lark, I picked up a bag of Kirkland brand dried blueberries during a Sunday afternoon trip to Costco. They're incredible! They turned out to be large, moist, and so sweet and fragrant that we started making a trip each month just to load up the truck.

A soft touch is required with this dough, so use your hands—not an electric mixer.

4 cups unbleached all-purpose flour, sifted, plus more for dusting

½ teaspoon kosher salt

½ cup granulated sugar

1 tablespoon plus 1 teaspoon baking powder

¾ cup (1½ sticks) unsalted butter, chilled and cubed

1½ cups dried blueberries

½ cup coarsely chopped crystallized ginger

2 large eggs

1¾ cups heavy cream

1 large egg, whisked with 1 tablespoon water

Turbinado sugar, for sprinkling

1. Preheat the oven to 375°F. Line a baking sheet with parchment paper.

2. In a large bowl, whisk together the flour, salt, granulated sugar, and baking powder. Cut the chilled cubed butter into the flour mixture with your fingers, two knives, or a pastry blender (not a mixer) until broken down into pea-sized pieces. Stir in the dried blueberries and crystallized ginger. Using a wooden spoon or your hands, mix in the eggs and cream until just combined. The dough should look dry, but should hold together and not flake.

3. Turn the dough out onto a lightly floured surface. Using your hands, gather it up into a pile and mix with your fingers. With the palms of your hands (or a rolling pin), flatten the dough into a roughly 8 x 11-inch rectangle about 1 inch tall.

4. Dip a sharp knife in flour and cut the large rectangle into 9 smaller rectangles, about 3 inches deep by 3½ inches wide. Cut each rectangle in half diagonally.

5. Place the scones on the prepared baking sheet about 1 inch apart. Brush the tops with the egg wash and sprinkle with turbinado sugar. Bake for 18 minutes, turning the pan halfway through until the tops are golden brown. Let cool completely on a raised wire rack. The scones will keep in a tightly sealed plastic bag at room temperature for up to a day, or in the freezer for up to 6 months.

Howdy Neighbor Muffins
WITH CRANBERRIES, ORANGE, AND WALNUTS

Makes 12 to 15 regular muffins or 8 to 10 jumbo muffins

A July vacation on Cape Cod years ago inspired these muffins. Early each morning, I biked over to a Portuguese bakery to buy their cranberry muffins, packed full of walnuts and a good hit of orange zest. I was working for the *Washington Post*, but promised myself that if I ever opened a bakery, I'd bake these every day. I did, and we do. Without a doubt, these muffins are our biggest seller; between our two locations and our online orders, in a good week we make nearly a thousand of these fist-sized bombs. I've been shipping these to my ninety-three-year-old aunt Molly in North Carolina any time she calls about them, and I think about her every time I see a batch come out of the oven.

The muffins at the bakery are jumbo-sized, but we've scaled back the recipe here to accommodate regular muffin tins. If you want to make the larger version, use a Texas-sized muffin pan and increase the baking time to 25 to 30 minutes.

Nonstick cooking spray

1 cup granulated sugar

Zest of 1 orange

3 cups unbleached all-purpose flour, sifted

1 tablespoon baking powder

½ teaspoon kosher salt

½ cup (1 stick) unsalted butter, melted

3 large eggs

¾ cup whole milk

Juice of 1 orange

1½ cups fresh or frozen cranberries

1½ cups walnut pieces

Turbinado sugar, for sprinkling

1. Preheat the oven to 375°F. Coat a muffin tin with nonstick spray and line it with paper liners (you may need two tins).

2. In a large bowl, mix together the granulated sugar and orange zest. Let sit for a few minutes to allow the orange flavor to infuse the sugar. Add the flour, baking powder, and salt and whisk to combine.

3. In a medium bowl, whisk together the melted butter, eggs, milk, and orange juice. Add the egg mixture to the flour mixture and stir just to combine. Do not overmix. Fold in the cranberries and walnuts.

4. Scoop the batter into the prepared muffin tin, filling each liner to the top. Generously sprinkle turbinado sugar over each muffin. Bake for 20 to 25 minutes, until light golden brown and a toothpick inserted into the center of a muffin comes out clean. Let cool slightly in the pan, then transfer the muffins to a raised wire rack to finish cooling.

Savory Stuffed Biscuits
WITH TOMATO AND MOZZARELLA

Makes 8 to 10 biscuits

These grab 'n' go goodies are popular for home brunches and picnics. The stuffed biscuits make a big impression, but take only a short amount of time to make. Treat the dough as a blank canvas and experiment with whatever ingredients you might have on hand or with seasonal standouts from your local farmer's market. This is my favorite variation during the summer—pesto, fresh basil, a slice of a local tomato, and a round of mozzarella cheese.

A soft touch is required with this dough, so use your hands—not an electric mixer.

BISCUITS:

3½ cups unbleached all-purpose flour, sifted, plus more as needed

1 tablespoon baking powder

¼ teaspoon baking soda

2 teaspoons kosher salt

2½ teaspoons sugar

½ cup vegetable shortening

½ cup (1 stick) unsalted butter, chilled and cubed, plus 4 tablespoons (½ stick), at room temperature

1 cup buttermilk

FILLING:

12 fresh basil leaves

12 medium tomato rounds, roughly 1½ inches across

12 buffalo mozzarella rounds, roughly 1½ inches across

¼ cup pesto

TOPPING:

1 large egg, whisked with 1 tablespoon water

1 cup shredded Parmesan cheese

Sea salt and freshly ground black pepper

1. Preheat the oven to 400°F. Line a baking sheet with parchment paper.

2. **Make the biscuits:** In a large bowl, whisk together the flour, baking powder, baking soda, salt, and sugar. Cut the shortening and the chilled cubed butter into the flour mixture with your fingers, two knives, or a pastry blender (not a mixer) until broken down into pea-sized pieces. Pour the buttermilk into the dry mixture all at once and, using a wooden spoon, fold in the buttermilk as quickly and as gently as possible. Flour your hands and reach into the bowl and under the dough and combine, flipping it around. Mix it up as gently as possible without being too tough on the dough. The dough will be sticky, but manageable. Add more flour if needed.

3. Turn the dough out onto a lightly floured surface and, working lightly, use your hands to pat the dough into a roughly 6 x 8-inch rectangle about ½ inch tall.

4. Arrange the dough so one long side is facing you and spread the bottom two-thirds of the dough with a third of the softened butter. Fold the unbuttered portion over so it covers half of the buttered side, and then fold over the other buttered side onto the unbuttered dough, creating three layers. Turn the dough a quarter, roll it out with a floured rolling pin into a 6 x 8-inch rectangle, and repeat the process twice more, using half of the remaining butter each time. Pat out the dough into a roughly 10 x 14-inch rectangle about ½ inch tall.

5. Dip a 3-inch biscuit cutter into flour and cut as many biscuits as you can from the dough, pressing straight down with the cutter each time (don't twist the cutter or the biscuits won't rise as well). Reroll the scraps as needed. Set half of the biscuits on the prepared baking sheet, spacing them about 1 inch apart. With your palm, press the biscuits down a bit.

6. **Fill the biscuits:** Place a basil leaf, a tomato round, a piece of mozzarella, and 1 teaspoon of the pesto at the center of each biscuit on the baking sheet. Press down on the remaining biscuits with your palm, making them a bit larger than the biscuits on the baking sheet. Place them over the filling, slightly pressing down with your palm. With your fingertip, gently press all around the edges to seal in the filling, but try not to crush the layers of dough you've formed.

7. Brush the tops with the egg wash. Cover the top of each biscuit with the Parmesan cheese, followed by some sea salt and pepper.

8. Bake for 15 minutes, turning the pan after 7 minutes, until the tops are golden brown. Transfer the biscuits to a raised wire rack to cool. The stuffed biscuits will keep in a tightly sealed plastic bag at room temperature for up to a day, or in the freezer for up to 6 months.

Red Truck Bakery Granola

Makes 12 cups

I want granola to have several layers of sweetness, a good crunch, and a real homemade taste—unlike anything available at a health food store—and it took a while to get this recipe just right. Each week, my neighbors smelled it wafting through my exhaust fan into their yards as I tried different variations (and they weighed in on their favorites after I left a bag on their doorstep as an apology). This hearty morning or snack-time favorite is packed with quick pick-me-up energy sources—chopped dates, golden raisins, dried blueberries, and cherries—as well as chunky proteins like walnuts, almonds, and sunflower seeds.

The Travel Channel's Andrew Zimmern says ours is the best granola in North America. Jane and Michael Stern of the wildly popular *Roadfood* went one step further and called it the best anywhere *in the world*.

Nonstick cooking spray
¾ cup sweetened shredded coconut
½ cup sliced almonds
½ cup coarsely chopped walnuts
½ cup hulled sunflower seeds
¼ teaspoon kosher salt
¼ cup packed light brown sugar
¼ teaspoon ground cinnamon
¼ cup canola oil
¾ cup pure maple syrup
¾ cup honey
1½ teaspoons pure vanilla extract
4½ cups old-fashioned rolled oats
½ cup dried blueberries
½ cup dried cherries
½ cup golden raisins
½ cup dark raisins
½ cup chopped dried dates

1. Preheat the oven to 250°F. Coat a rimmed baking sheet with nonstick spray.

2. In a large bowl, stir together the coconut, almonds, walnuts, and sunflower seeds.

3. In a separate large bowl, whisk together the salt, brown sugar, and cinnamon. Mix in the canola oil, maple syrup, honey, and vanilla. Add the wet mixture to the dry mixture and combine thoroughly using your hands. Add the oats and combine thoroughly.

4. Spread the wet granola mixture over the prepared baking sheet and bake for 15 minutes. Remove from the oven and stir. Bake for 15 minutes more and stir again. Use the bottom of a small saucepan to evenly flatten the granola. Bake for 10 minutes more, until the granola is a deep nut-brown color. Let cool completely.

5. Break the sheet of granola into small clusters into a large bowl. Add the dried blueberries, dried cherries, golden raisins, dark raisins, and dates and mix thoroughly, breaking up the clusters of granola into bite-size pieces.

6. Store the granola in airtight containers or resealable bags at room temperature for up to a week.

Sweet Stuffed Biscuits
with PEAR AND GOAT CHEESE

Makes 8 to 10 biscuits

Pear lavished with honey gives these stuffed biscuits an autumnal sweetness, while the goat cheese and fresh rosemary add more savory tones to balance it all out. This recipe takes our biscuits to the next level, and a basket of these is great for brunches, neighborly events, and church outings. These are a good afternoon partner to a cup of hot tea or coffee.

A soft touch is required with this dough, so use your hands—not an electric mixer.

BISCUITS:

3½ cups unbleached all-purpose flour, sifted, plus more as needed

1 tablespoon baking powder

¼ teaspoon baking soda

2 teaspoons kosher salt

3 tablespoons granulated sugar

½ cup vegetable shortening

½ cup (1 stick) unsalted butter, chilled and cubed, plus 4 tablespoons (½ stick), at room temperature

1 cup buttermilk

FILLING:

1 tablespoon chopped fresh rosemary

¼ teaspoon freshly ground black pepper

1½ large pears, peeled, cored, and cut into medium dice (about 1 cup)

1 tablespoon honey

1½ tablespoons goat cheese, at room temperature

TOPPING:

1 large egg, whisked with 1 tablespoon water

Freshly ground black pepper

Turbinado sugar, for sprinkling

1. Preheat the oven to 400°F. Line a baking sheet with parchment paper.

2. Make the biscuits: In a large bowl, whisk together the flour, baking powder, baking soda, salt, and granulated sugar. Cut the shortening and the chilled cubed butter into the flour mixture with your fingers, two knives, or a pastry blender (not a mixer) until broken down into pea-sized pieces. Pour the buttermilk into the dry mixture all at once and, using a wooden spoon, fold in the buttermilk as quickly and as gently as possible. Flour your hands and reach into the bowl and under the dough and combine, flipping it around. Mix it up as gently as possible without being too tough on the dough. The dough will be sticky, but manageable. Add more flour if needed.

3. Turn the dough out onto a lightly floured surface and, working lightly, use your hands to pat the dough into a roughly 6 x 8-inch rectangle about ½ inch tall.

4. Arrange the dough so one long side is facing you and spread the bottom two-thirds of the dough with a third of the softened butter. Fold the unbuttered portion over so it covers half of the buttered side, and then fold over the other buttered side onto the unbuttered dough, creating three layers. Turn the dough a quarter, roll it out with a floured rolling pin into a 6 x 8-inch rectangle, and repeat the process twice more, using half of the remaining butter each time. Pat out the dough into a roughly 10 x 14-inch rectangle about ½ inch tall.

5. Dip a 3-inch biscuit cutter into flour and cut as many biscuits as you can from the dough, pressing straight down with the cutter each time (don't twist the cutter or the biscuits won't rise as well). Reroll the scraps as needed. Set half of the biscuits

on the prepared baking sheet, spacing them about 1 inch apart. With your palm, press the biscuits down a bit to make them a little wider, about 3¼ inches. With the edge of your palm, push into the center of the biscuit to create a shallow indent (being careful to keep the edges high).

6. Make the filling: In a medium bowl, combine the rosemary and pepper. Add the pears and the honey. Let sit for a few minutes, then transfer to a plate lined with a few paper towels to soak up excess liquid.

7. Place ½ teaspoon of goat cheese in the center of each of the biscuits on the baking sheet. Place 2 tablespoons of the pear filling over the goat cheese, avoiding the edges of the biscuit.

8. Press down on the remaining biscuits with your palm, making them a bit larger than the biscuits on the baking sheet. Place them over the pear filling. With your fingertip, gently press all around the edges to seal the filling, but try not to crush the layers of dough you've formed.

9. Brush the tops lightly with the egg wash. Generously sprinkle with pepper and turbinado sugar.

10. Bake for about 15 minutes, turning the pan after 10 minutes, until the tops are golden brown. Place on a raised wire rack to cool. The stuffed biscuits will keep in a tightly sealed plastic bag at room temperature for up to a day, or in the freezer for up to 6 months.

Barnyard Breakfast Pie

Makes one 10-inch pie

For this hearty breakfast pie, we start by crumbling up leftover Rise and Shine Biscuits and placing them in the bottom of a piecrust with big chunks of sausage and hearty bits of smoked bacon. We drown it all in an egg mixture amped up with Aunt Darla's Smoky Pimento Cheese and bake until the top is golden brown and puffed up. It's the perfect fuel on weekend mornings before hiking in the Blue Ridge Mountains or tubing down the North Fork of the Shenandoah River.

½ recipe Savory Pie and Quiche Crust dough (page 102), or 1 store-bought crust

About 5 Rise and Shine Biscuits (page 24, or use store-bought), broken into large pieces and lightly toasted (3 cups)

12 scallions, coarsely chopped

2 (4-ounce) breakfast sausage patties, cooked and broken up into large pieces (about 2 cups)

6 bacon slices, cooked and coarsely chopped

6 large eggs, beaten

1 cup half-and-half

½ teaspoon kosher salt

½ teaspoon freshly ground black pepper

1 tablespoon red pepper flakes

5 tablespoons Aunt Darla's Smoky Pimento Cheese (page 198, or use store-bought)

2 tablespoons Rooster's Pepper Jelly (page 195, or use store-bought), heated until thin and runny

1. Preheat the oven to 400°F.

2. Roll out the pie dough into a 13-inch round, fit it into a 10-inch pie pan, trim, and crimp the edges.

3. Scatter the toasted biscuit pieces into the pie shell and sprinkle evenly with the scallions. Add the sausage and bacon.

4. In a medium bowl, whisk together the eggs, half-and-half, salt, black pepper, and red pepper flakes. Add the pimento cheese and whisk to combine, then pour the mixture into the pie shell, making sure not to fill it past the bottom of the crimped edges. With a spoon, quickly ladle the melted pepper jelly across the top.

5. Bake for 20 minutes. Reduce the oven temperature to 375°F, turn the pie pan, and bake for 10 to 20 minutes more, until the top is golden brown and the egg mixture is firm. Let cool before slicing and serving.

Sausage and Jalapeño Scones

Makes 12 scones

We love traditional sausage biscuits—thick, round, just-out-of-the-oven golden pillows sliced in half, packed with a thick patty of breakfast sausage, and slathered with pepper jelly. This version mixes all those components together and adds pickled jalapeños for a smidgen of spiciness in a great portable breakfast bite.

We have the good fortune to be able to get freshly ground breakfast sausage from our friends at the Whole Ox butcher shop across the road. You can pick up breakfast sausage from your local butcher, although a mix of Jimmy Dean's sage and hot varieties is a pretty good choice, too.

A soft touch is required with this dough, so use your hands—not an electric mixer.

1 pound breakfast sausage

4 cups unbleached all-purpose flour, sifted, plus more as needed

1 tablespoon plus 1 teaspoon baking powder

1½ teaspoons baking soda

1½ teaspoons kosher salt, plus a pinch

½ cup vegetable shortening

¼ cup chopped pickled jalapeños

¼ cup **Rooster's Pepper Jelly** (page 195, or use store-bought)

1½ cups buttermilk

3 tablespoons unsalted butter, at room temperature, plus 2 tablespoons, melted

1. Preheat the oven to 300°F.

2. Remove the breakfast sausage from its casings. On a clean cutting board, divide the sausage into two mounds and flatten each down with your palms to create patties. Place them on a baking sheet and bake for 15 minutes. Flip the patties and bake for 15 to 20 minutes more, until the middle of the patties show no sign of pink. Let cool, then use your hands to break the patties into ½-inch pieces.

3. Increase the oven temperature to 400°F. Line a baking sheet with parchment paper. Line a portion of your work surface with newspaper and set a raised wire rack on top.

4. In a large bowl, whisk together the flour, baking powder, baking soda, and salt. Cut the shortening into the flour mixture with your fingers, two knives, or a pastry blender (not a mixer) until broken down into pea-sized pieces. Add the cooked sausage and jalapeños.

5. In a medium bowl, stir together the pepper jelly and the buttermilk. Pour the buttermilk mixture into the dry mixture all at once and, using a wooden spoon, fold in the buttermilk as quickly and as gently as possible. The dough will be sticky, but manageable. Add more flour if needed.

6. Turn the dough out onto a lightly floured surface and, working lightly, use your hands to pat the dough into a roughly 9 x 12-inch rectangle about ¾ inch tall.

7. Arrange the dough so one long side is facing you and spread 1 tablespoon of the softened butter over the bottom half. Fold the unbuttered half over the buttered half. Turn the dough a quarter and, using your palms, press the dough out to half its thickness. Repeat the process twice more, using half the remaining softened butter each time. Pat the dough into a roughly 8 x 10-inch rectangle about ¾ inch tall.

8. Dip a 3-inch biscuit cutter into flour and cut as many scones as you can from the dough, pressing straight down with the cutter each time (don't twist the cutter or the scones won't rise as well). Reroll the scraps as needed.

9. Place the scones on the prepared baking sheet and bake for 14 minutes, turning the baking sheet halfway through, until the tops are light golden brown.

10. Meanwhile, in a small bowl, stir together the melted butter and a pinch of salt.

11. Transfer the scones to the wire rack and brush the tops with the salted melted butter. The scones will keep in a tightly sealed plastic bag at room temperature for up to a day, or in the freezer for up to 6 months.

Holler Doughnuts

Makes 12 to 15 doughnuts

Driving through the canyons and hollows (hollers) in the Shenandoah foothills, we always keep an eye out for two local foods: pepperoni rolls and doughnuts. We've made both at the bakery, although we're not crazy about frying things because no one wants to spend the rest of the day smelling like grease. Luckily, it turns out, this sweet yeast batter—based on our brioche and king cake dough—makes a darned good baked doughnut. We've topped it with a glaze made from Travis and Joyce Miller's Falling Bark Farm hickory syrup, which is produced near us in Berryville, Virginia, but pure maple syrup works great.

DOUGHNUTS:

1 cup whole milk, warmed

½ cup plus 1 teaspoon granulated sugar

1 tablespoon active dry yeast

½ teaspoon lemon zest

½ teaspoon orange zest

4 tablespoons (½ stick) unsalted butter, at room temperature, plus more for greasing

1 large egg

1 teaspoon pure vanilla extract

1 teaspoon kosher salt

½ teaspoon ground mace, or ground or freshly grated nutmeg

4 cups unbleached all-purpose flour, sifted, plus more as needed

CANDIED PECANS:

½ cup granulated sugar

½ cup packed dark brown sugar

1 teaspoon kosher salt

1 tablespoon ground cinnamon

½ teaspoon cayenne pepper

1 large egg white

½ teaspoon pure vanilla extract

1½ cups unsalted pecan halves

GLAZE:

1½ cups confectioners' sugar

½ cup hickory syrup (we like Falling Bark Farm) or pure maple syrup

1. Make the doughnuts: In a small bowl, whisk together the milk, 1 teaspoon of the granulated sugar, and the yeast. Let stand for 10 minutes until foamy.

2. In a separate small bowl, combine the remaining ½ cup granulated sugar, the lemon zest, and the orange zest. Let sit for a few minutes to allow the citrus flavor to infuse the sugar.

3. In the bowl of a stand mixer fitted with the paddle attachment, combine the sugar-zest mixture and the butter and beat on medium-high speed until light and fluffy, about 2 minutes. Add the yeast mixture and beat until just combined. Add the egg and vanilla and mix until combined.

4. In a medium bowl, whisk together the salt, mace, and flour until combined. With the mixer running on low speed, add a third of the flour mixture and beat thoroughly to combine. Scrape down the sides and bottom of the bowl with a spatula. Add another third of the flour mixture and beat on low speed to combine. Place the dough hook on your mixer, then add the remaining flour mixture and mix for 3 minutes on low speed, until the dough gathers on the hook and pulls away from the sides of the bowl. Keep kneading on medium-high speed for 8 minutes.

(recipe continues)

5. Turn the dough out onto a clean surface and knead it with your hands, flipping the dough over and over until its surface is smooth. Add more flour, a bit at a time, if needed (the dough should be soft, but not goopy).

6. Grease a large bowl with butter, place the dough in the bowl, and cover with a damp towel. Let sit in a warm, draft-free place for 1 hour, until doubled in size.

7. Turn the dough out onto a floured work surface and roll it out to a thickness of about ½ inch. Using a 4-inch biscuit cutter, cut as many rounds as you can from the dough, pressing straight down with the cutter each time (don't twist the cutter or the doughnuts won't rise as well). Use a 1-inch round cutter to remove the center of each doughnut (again pressing straight down without twisting each time). Gather up the dough scraps, including the holes, and let rest for 5 minutes. Roll out the scraps to ½-inch thickness and cut more doughnuts. Line a baking sheet with parchment paper and place the doughnuts on the baking sheet. Let rise in a warm, draft-free place for 30 to 60 minutes, until doubled in size.

8. While the doughnuts rise, make the candied pecans: Preheat the oven to 300°F. Line a baking sheet with parchment paper. Set a raised wire rack inside another baking sheet.

9. In a medium bowl, whisk together the granulated sugar, brown sugar, salt, cinnamon, and cayenne.

10. In a separate medium bowl, whisk together the egg white, vanilla, and 1 teaspoon water until frothy. Add the pecans and toss to coat well. Add the sugar mixture and toss again until the pecans are completely covered.

11. Spread the pecans on the parchment-lined baking sheet and bake for 45 minutes, tossing every 15 minutes, until the coating has hardened and is dark brown. Let cool for a few minutes before coarsely chopping.

12. Increase the oven temperature to 400°F.

13. Make the glaze: In a medium bowl, whisk together the confectioners' sugar, hickory syrup, and ½ cup water. The glaze should be very thin. Add more water, 1 teaspoon at a time, if necessary.

14. Bake the doughnuts for 12 to 15 minutes, until golden brown and puffy. Let cool for a few minutes. While still warm, dip the top of each doughnut into the glaze, then scatter the pecan pieces on top and place on the wire rack while the glaze sets.

Maple-Glazed Pumpkin Scones
WITH RAISINS

Makes 12 to 16 scones

The route from our bakery in Marshall to Little Washington, Virginia, is one of the most beautiful autumn drives in America (even *Time* magazine says so). The road winds through the countryside, slipping down long slopes, through hollows and over small hills dotted with round hay bales, horses, and cattle. The fall leaves provide a natural fireworks show as they explode with sizzling reds, bright yellows, and brilliant oranges.

A sea of brake lights complements that colorful display as locals and visitors alike take in the scenery. Many of them stop at our bakery to grab some goodies to take home. One of the most popular items in the case at that time of year is our maple-glazed pumpkin scones, which embody the tastes of the season.

A soft touch is required with this dough, so use your hands—not an electric mixer.

SCONES:

6 cups unbleached all-purpose flour, sifted, plus more for dusting

½ cup packed dark brown sugar

1½ teaspoons orange zest

1 tablespoon plus 1½ teaspoons baking powder

¼ teaspoon kosher salt

½ teaspoon ground cinnamon

¼ teaspoon ground ginger

¼ teaspoon ground or freshly grated nutmeg

¼ teaspoon ground cloves

½ cup (1 stick) unsalted butter, chilled and cubed

1½ cups dark raisins

2 large eggs

½ cup heavy cream

1 cup pure pumpkin puree

1 large egg, whisked with 1 tablespoon water (optional)

Turbinado sugar, for sprinkling (optional)

MAPLE GLAZE:

2 cups confectioners' sugar

5 drops pure maple extract, or 1 tablespoon pure maple syrup

1. Preheat the oven to 375°F. Line a portion of your work surface with newspaper and set a raised wire rack on top. Line a baking sheet with parchment paper.

2. Make the scones: In a large bowl, whisk together the flour, brown sugar, orange zest, baking powder, salt, cinnamon, ginger, nutmeg, and cloves. Cut the chilled cubed butter into the flour mixture with your fingers, two knives, or a pastry blender (not a mixer) until broken down into pea-sized pieces. Stir in the raisins.

3. In a medium bowl, whisk together the eggs, cream, and pumpkin, then add the egg mixture to the flour mixture and mix until well combined.

4. Turn the dough out onto a lightly floured surface. Using your hands, gather it up into a pile and mix with your fingers. It will be a little dry and crumbly; it shouldn't be a wet dough. Press down on the dough with your palms to form it into a rough pile. With the palms of your hands (or a rolling pin), flatten the dough into a 9 x 12-inch rectangle about 1¼ inches tall.

(recipe continues)

5. Dip a 3-inch biscuit cutter into flour and cut as many scones as you can from the dough, pressing straight down with the cutter each time (don't twist the cutter or the scones won't rise as well). Reroll the scraps as needed.

6. Place the scones on the prepared baking sheet about 1 inch apart. If desired, brush the tops with the egg wash and sprinkle with turbinado sugar. Bake for 20 to 25 minutes, turning the pan halfway through, until the tops are golden brown. Transfer the scones to the wire rack and let cool completely before glazing.

7. Meanwhile, make the maple glaze: In a small bowl, mix together the confectioners' sugar, maple extract, and 1 tablespoon water. Add more water a teaspoon at a time until you have a thick but pourable frosting.

8. With a fork, squeeze bottle, or your fingertips, drizzle the frosting across the scones in a zigzag pattern. Let the frosting set before devouring. The scones will keep in a tightly sealed plastic bag at room temperature for up to a day, or in the freezer for up to 6 months.

Apple Orchard Muffins

Makes 12 to 15 regular muffins or 8 to 10 jumbo muffins

When Dwight and I first bought our Virginia Piedmont farmhouse, we went nearly every summer weekend, but it turns out fall was even better. We'd stop at the orchards to pick up white-handled paper bags full of apples for baking projects at the farmhouse, including these apple muffins based on a *Country Living* magazine recipe I remember making as a kid.

We're lucky to be in the middle of the Shenandoah Valley, surrounded by apple orchards offering up Honeycrisp, Mutsu, Winesap, Stayman, Rome, and Golden Delicious varieties. I tend to use several types in our baked goods, though Granny Smiths always work in a pinch.

The muffins at the bakery are jumbo-sized, but we've scaled back the recipe here to accommodate regular muffin tins. If you want to make the larger version, use a Texas-sized muffin pan and increase the baking time to 25 to 30 minutes.

Nonstick cooking spray

1 cup packed dark brown sugar

½ cup sorghum syrup or honey

½ cup plus 2 tablespoons vegetable oil

1 large egg

1½ teaspoons pure vanilla extract

2¾ cups unbleached all-purpose flour, sifted

¼ teaspoon ground cinnamon

1 teaspoon baking soda

½ teaspoon baking powder

¼ teaspoon kosher salt

1 cup buttermilk

2 cups coarsely chopped (½-inch pieces) peeled apples (from about 2 large apples)

1 cup golden raisins

Turbinado sugar, for sprinkling

1. Preheat the oven to 350°F. Coat a muffin tin with nonstick spray and line it with paper liners (you may need two tins). Lightly spray the liners as well.

2. In a large bowl, whisk together the brown sugar, sorghum syrup, vegetable oil, egg, and vanilla.

3. In a separate large bowl, whisk together the flour, cinnamon, baking soda, baking powder, and salt. Stir half the sugar mixture into the flour mixture. Add the buttermilk and mix well with a spatula. Add the remaining sugar mixture and stir to combine completely. Fold in the chopped apples and the golden raisins. Scoop the batter into the prepared muffin tin, filling the liners to the top. Generously sprinkle turbinado sugar over each muffin.

4. Bake for 20 to 25 minutes, until light golden brown and a toothpick inserted into the center of a muffin comes out clean. Let cool slightly in the pan, then transfer the muffins to a raised wire rack to finish cooling.

RED TRUCK BAKERY COOKBOOK

Ham Scones
WITH CHEDDAR AND SCALLIONS

Makes 12 scones

When we first opened the bakery, we offered up traditional Southern ham biscuits: baked biscuits sliced in half and layered with country ham and pepper jelly. They became too popular too fast and we couldn't keep up with the demand. To save prep time and get these out front by the time we opened in the mornings, we instead started mixing all the ingredients together into the dough. These fluffy scones sport generous chunks of country ham, gooey pockets of melted Cheddar, and spicy chopped scallions. They're a special treat for our customers because we only sell them on the weekends.

A soft touch is required with this dough, so use your hands—not an electric mixer.

3½ cups unbleached all-purpose flour, sifted, plus more for dusting

2½ teaspoons baking powder

¼ teaspoon baking soda

1 teaspoon kosher salt, plus a pinch

1 teaspoon sugar

1 cup (2 sticks) unsalted butter, chilled and cubed, plus 2 tablespoons, melted

1 cup buttermilk

1½ cups coarsely chopped (1-inch pieces) country ham (about ½ pound)

8 scallions, sliced into ¼-inch-wide pieces

2 cups grated Cheddar cheese

1. Preheat the oven to 400°F. Line a baking sheet with parchment paper. Line a portion of your work surface with newspaper and set a raised wire rack on top.

2. In a large bowl, whisk together the flour, baking powder, baking soda, salt, and sugar. Cut the chilled cubed butter into the flour mixture with your fingers, two knives, or a pastry blender (not a mixer) until broken down into pea-sized pieces. Pour the buttermilk into the dry mixture all at once and, using a wooden spoon, fold in the buttermilk as quickly and as gently as possible. Add the ham, scallions, and cheese and gently mix until completely incorporated. Flour your hands and reach into the bowl and under the dough and combine, flipping it around. Mix it up as gently as possible without being too tough on the dough. The dough will be sticky, but manageable. Add more flour if needed.

3. Turn the dough out onto a lightly floured surface and, working lightly, use your hands to pat the dough into a roughly 8 x 10-inch rectangle about ¾ inch thick.

4. Dip a 3-inch biscuit cutter into flour and cut as many scones as you can from the dough, pressing straight down with the cutter each time (don't twist the cutter or the scones won't rise as well). Reroll the scraps as needed. Place the scones on the prepared baking sheet and bake for 15 to 20 minutes, turning the pan after 7 minutes, until the tops are light golden brown.

5. Meanwhile, in a small bowl, mix the 2 tablespoons melted butter with a pinch of salt.

6. Transfer the scones to the wire rack and brush their tops with the salted melted butter. The scones will keep in a tightly sealed plastic bag at room temperature for up to a day, or in the freezer for up to 6 months.

Guava Pastelitos

Makes 20 pastelitos

A friend for over three decades, my neighbor Barry Dixon is not only an acclaimed international interior designer—his work is regularly featured in *Architectural Digest* and coffee table books—but also a *pastelito* connoisseur. The Cuban turnovers feature flaky puff pastry enveloping a sweet, tangy, and tropical mix of guava paste and cream cheese. They go down well with a couple of *café Cubanos*. After Barry talked for years about snacking on pastelitos during trips to Miami, he insisted I try my hand at them—not necessarily to sell, but to bake for him. Turns out they're very easy to make, so you can knock them out—and fire up a few *cafés—muy rápido.*

Remove the puff pastry from the freezer and let it thaw in the fridge overnight. You want it slightly chilled, but not frozen, when you're working with it; it's made up of many buttered layers so you don't want it to warm up too much or else the layers will mash together as the butter melts.

1 (1-pound) package puff pastry (2 sheets), thawed

1 (14-ounce) bar guava paste (about 1 cup)

1 (8-ounce) package cream cheese, at room temperature

1 large egg, whisked with 1 tablespoon water

Turbinado sugar, for sprinkling

1. Preheat the oven to 400°F. Line two baking sheets with parchment paper.

2. Cut each sheet of puff pastry into ten 3-inch squares. Place the squares on the prepared baking sheets.

3. In the bowl of a stand mixer fitted with the paddle attachment, beat together the guava paste and cream cheese on medium speed for 5 minutes, until well combined and smooth.

4. Place 1 heaping tablespoon of the guava–cream cheese mixture in the center of each pastry square. (You will have extra filling, which is great for spreading on Rise and Shine Biscuits, page 24. It will keep for one week in the refrigerator.) Carefully brush the outer edges of the pastry squares with the egg wash. Fold the pastry over the filling to form a triangle. With a fork, press the edges to seal.

5. Brush the tops of the pastelitos with the egg wash, sprinkle with turbinado sugar, and make three diagonal slits in the tops with a sharp knife.

6. Bake for 18 to 25 minutes, until the tops are golden brown and puffed. Transfer to a wire rack and let cool completely before eating; the filling will be very hot.

Sweet Pies and a Buckle

Southern Shoofly Pie
WITH SORGHUM

Makes one 10-inch pie

When I first moved to the DC area, I spent weekends taking road trips to explore the mid-Atlantic region, including Pennsylvania's Amish country. I'd return home with a bag of sweet smoked bologna and at least two molasses-rich, crumb-topped shoofly pies.

A couple of years ago, a customer asked if we made shoofly pie at the Red Truck. We didn't, but it inspired me to create one that's more Fauquier County than Lancaster County. Sweetened with a mellower sorghum syrup, adorned with broken-up pieces of cakes, and topped with smoked sugar, it's a little lighter than its Keystone State cousin.

½ recipe **Classic Piecrust dough (page 60)**, or 1 store-bought crust

CRUMB TOPPING:

¾ cup unbleached all-purpose flour, sifted

¼ cup packed dark brown sugar

4 tablespoons (½ stick) unsalted butter, chilled and cubed

½ teaspoon ground cinnamon

1 cup crumbled Meyer Lemon Cake (page 132) or pound cake

FILLING:

2 cups loosely packed crumbled Meyer Lemon Cake (page 132) or pound cake

¾ cup sorghum syrup

¼ cup honey

½ teaspoon baking soda

½ cup boiling water

3 tablespoons unsalted butter, melted

1 teaspoon pure vanilla extract

2 large eggs, at room temperature

¼ cup packed light brown sugar

¼ cup smoked sugar (I like Bourbon Barrel Foods) or turbinado sugar

1½ teaspoons orange zest

1 teaspoon lemon zest

¼ teaspoon kosher salt

1. Preheat the oven to 425°F. Place a raised wire rack inside a rimmed baking sheet.

2. Roll out the pie dough into a 13-inch round, fit it into a 10-inch pie pan, trim, and crimp the edges.

3. Make the crumb topping: In the bowl of a stand mixer fitted with the paddle attachment, combine the flour, dark brown sugar, butter, and cinnamon and mix on low speed, just until pea-sized lumps form. Avoid overmixing; the topping will quickly turn into an unusable paste. With the mixer running on low speed, mix in the cake pieces until just combined.

4. Make the filling: Evenly scatter the crumbled cake pieces over the crust.

5. In a large bowl, combine the sorghum syrup, honey, and baking soda. Pour in the boiling water; whisk until combined (it will foam up, then subside). Whisk in the melted butter and vanilla. Add the eggs one at a time, whisking until well mixed after each addition. Add the light brown sugar, smoked sugar, orange zest, lemon zest, and salt and mix well. Pour the mixture over the cake chunks in the pie shell, making sure not to fill it past the bottom of the crimped edges.

6. Evenly sprinkle the crumb topping over the filling. Carefully place the pie on the prepared baking sheet. Bake for 15 minutes, then reduce the oven temperature to 350°F and turn the pie. Bake for 20 minutes more, until the filling is firm and golden. Let cool on a raised wire rack.

MEET OUR PRODUCERS

Compass Winds
Sorghum

PAGE 214

Wild Raspberry Buckle

Makes one 9-inch buckle

Old-timey and nearly unknown baked treats like slumps, grunts, pandowdies, and buckles fascinate me. A buckle, I've discovered, is a cross between a coffee cake and a cobbler. Fruit is pressed down into the buttery dough to create a landscape of hills and hollows. A hearty scattering of turbinado sugar across the top adds a solid crunch, while simultaneously protecting the fruit from being burned by the heat of the oven. Though I like using wild raspberries freshly picked from the brambles on the north end of our farm, you can make this recipe with almost any fruit. Strawberries, cherries, peaches, and blackberries work just as well—and feel free to combine several kinds, as we do when new seasonal crops arrive at the bakery.

Nonstick cooking spray

2½ cups raspberries

2 cups plus 1 tablespoon unbleached all-purpose flour, sifted

1 cup granulated sugar

1 tablespoon lemon zest

½ cup (1 stick) unsalted butter, at room temperature

1 large egg, at room temperature

2 teaspoons baking powder

¾ teaspoon kosher salt

¼ cup buttermilk

½ cup heavy cream

½ tablespoon pure vanilla extract

Turbinado sugar, for sprinkling

1. Preheat the oven to 350°F. Coat a 9-inch round cake pan with nonstick spray.

2. In small bowl, mix the raspberries with 1 tablespoon of the flour, stirring to coat evenly.

3. In the bowl of a stand mixer fitted with the paddle attachment, combine the granulated sugar and lemon zest. Let sit for a few minutes to allow the lemon flavor to infuse the sugar. Add the butter and beat on medium speed until well combined and pale yellow, about 3 minutes. Add the egg and beat until just combined.

4. In a medium bowl, whisk together the remaining 2 cups flour, the baking powder, and the salt.

5. In a spouted measuring cup, mix together the buttermilk, cream, and vanilla.

6. Add the flour mixture to the butter mixture in three additions, alternating with the buttermilk mixture and beginning and ending with the flour; beat well on medium speed after each addition.

7. Spoon the cake batter into the prepared pan but leave it rough and mounded and not smoothed out. Distribute the raspberries evenly, pressing them halfway down into the batter. Sprinkle a good amount of turbinado sugar evenly across the top.

8. Bake for 45 minutes, until golden brown and a toothpick inserted into the center comes out clean. Let cool slightly, then serve directly from the pan.

Chester's Peach Pie
with GINGER

Makes one 10-inch pie

The middle of July heralds the beginning of peach season, which runs through Labor Day. I buy ours from Chester Hess, a third-generation grower just across the state line in Martinsburg, West Virginia. He sets aside blue-ribbon peaches, but we also crave the fruit that has been banged up a bit, because ugly fruit still makes beautiful pies. Plus, they're pretty juicy and they're sold at a discount.

The key to this recipe is freestone peaches, which usually hit the farmer's market in midsummer. Unlike the earlier-peaking cling peach, the pit of the freestone peach slides right out when you halve the fruit. I've learned that a paring knife works best for quick peeling, although some prefer to blanch the peaches quickly in a pot of boiling water and slip the fuzzy exterior off when cooled.

8 cups sliced peeled peaches (about 12)

7 tablespoons cornstarch

1 cup sugar

1 teaspoon ground cinnamon

⅛ teaspoon ground or freshly grated nutmeg

1 tablespoon finely chopped crystallized ginger

Juice of ½ lemon

1 recipe Classic Piecrust dough (page 60), or 2 store-bought crusts

2 tablespoons unsalted butter, chilled and cubed

1 large egg, whisked with 1 tablespoon water

1. Preheat the oven to 375 °F. Place a raised wire rack inside a rimmed baking sheet.

2. In a large saucepan, combine 2 cups of the peaches, the cornstarch, sugar, cinnamon, nutmeg, and ginger. Bring to a boil over medium heat, then add the lemon juice. Remove the pan from the heat and set aside to cool. Add the remaining 6 cups peaches and stir to mix completely.

3. Roll out one disc of pie dough into a 13-inch round, fit it into a 10-inch pie pan, trim, and crimp the edges. Pour the peach mixture into the crust and dot the top of the fruit with the butter.

4. Roll out the second disc of dough into a roughly 18 x 13-inch rectangle. Cut it crosswise into six 3 x 13-inch strips.

5. Create a lattice crust by laying three strips of dough across the pie horizontally, then laying three strips of dough perpendicularly across them. Weave the top strips of dough over and under those on the bottom. Trim the dough about 2 inches from the pan, and roll and crimp the edges, combining the lattice crust with the dough in the pan. Brush the dough with the egg wash.

6. Carefully place the pie on the prepared baking sheet. Bake for 1 hour to 1 hour 15 minutes, turning the baking sheet after 30 minutes, until the center is bubbling. Let cool completely on a raised wire rack before serving.

Caramel Pumpkin Pie

Makes one 10-inch pie

In 2011, *Washingtonian* magazine blind-taste-tested more than twenty pies in the Washington, DC, area—and our Caramel Pumpkin took home the top prize! Instead of simply adding white sugar to the mix, we make a golden caramel sauce to sweeten the pie. A word of warning: the caramel goes from brown to burnt very quickly, so stay focused while it's cooking. Every Thanksgiving, we inevitably have to dump burnt batches of it because we become distracted. As for the pumpkin portion of the pie, we used to roast them and make a puree. Even after all that work, though, it was never as good as pure pumpkin puree from a can. So that's what we use, and you should, too.

½ recipe Classic Piecrust dough (page 60), or
   1 store-bought crust

1 cup sugar

2 cups heavy cream, at room temperature

1 (15-ounce) can pure pumpkin puree

1½ teaspoons ground ginger

1¼ teaspoons ground cinnamon

¼ teaspoon ground or freshly grated nutmeg

Pinch of ground cloves

½ teaspoon kosher salt

4 large eggs

1. Roll out the pie dough into a 13-inch round, fit it into in a 10-inch pie pan, trim, and crimp the edges. Chill in the refrigerator for 1 hour.

2. In a large saucepan, whisk together the sugar and ¼ cup plus 2 tablespoons water. Bring to a boil over high heat, but don't stir; gently swirl the pan on the burner and occasionally brush down the sides of the pan with a wet pastry brush. Cook until deep golden brown in color, 10 minutes or longer,

taking care not to burn it. Reduce the heat to low, add the cream (be careful, as it may splatter), and gently whisk it into the caramel until completely incorporated. Remove the pan from the heat and let it cool a bit.

3. Preheat the oven to 325°F with a rack in the center. Place a raised wire rack inside a rimmed baking sheet.

4. In the bowl of a stand mixer fitted with the whisk attachment, combine the pumpkin, ginger, cinnamon, nutmeg, cloves, and salt. Whisk on medium speed until combined, about 1 minute. Add the eggs one at a time and beat until combined. Scrape down the sides of the bowl with a rubber spatula as needed.

5. Pour the cooled caramel through a fine-mesh strainer into the mixer bowl to remove any sugar crystals. Beat on medium-high speed until everything is smoothly combined, stopping to scrape down the sides of the bowl as needed, 2 to 3 minutes. Pour the pumpkin mixture into the chilled pie shell, making sure not to fill it past the bottom of the crimped edges.

6. Carefully place the pie on the prepared baking sheet. Bake for 10 minutes and then increase the oven temperature to 350°F. Bake for 45 to 55 minutes more, gently turning the baking sheet after 25 minutes, until the filling is puffed and firm to about 2 inches from the rim. Don't worry if the center is jiggly; it'll finish baking while cooling. Let cool completely on a raised wire rack.

Classic Piecrust

Makes dough for two 10-inch crusts

Unless indicated otherwise, this crust is the foundation of every pie in this chapter. Though it's relatively traditional, we incorporate a little bit of lemon and orange zests as a subtle counterpoint to the dough's sweet, buttery flavor. After our customers enjoy our pies, they often compliment the crust. "There's something in there that I can't put my finger on, but I love it," they'll say. Now you know our secret.

For a lot of bakers who are just starting out, crafting the perfect crust can feel like an insurmountable challenge. Stop stressing. It can take time to get the method just right, but it's easier than you think. Simply roll out the dough about 3 inches larger than your pie pan and drape it loosely over it. Don't stretch the dough—if you do, it will shrink back in the oven and you won't be happy with the result. Fill the pie shell, cover the top with a second round of dough, and crimp the edges by pushing the dough with one thumb into the thumb and first finger of your other hand. Big, rustic crimping is what I like—with the amount of fruit inside and the weight of the pie, we don't want them looking dainty.

3½ cups unbleached all-purpose flour, sifted

1 teaspoon kosher salt

2 tablespoons plus 1 teaspoon sugar

¾ cup (1½ sticks) unsalted butter, chilled and cubed

¼ cup vegetable shortening, chilled

1 large egg yolk

1½ teaspoons orange zest

1½ teaspoons lemon zest

½ cup cold water, plus more as needed

1. In a large bowl, whisk together the flour, salt, and sugar. Add the chilled cubed butter and shortening; cut the butter and shortening into the flour mixture using your fingers, two knives, or a pastry blender, until broken down into pea-sized pieces. (Alternatively, combine the flour, salt, and sugar in a food processor, add the butter and shortening, and pulse until broken down into pea-sized pieces.) Add the egg yolk and the orange and lemon zests and mix by hand until combined (if you're using a food processor, transfer the mixture to a bowl before adding the egg yolk and zests). Gradually add the cold water and mix until the dough comes together. If it's crumbly, add a bit more water 1 teaspoon at a time.

2. Divide the dough in half and form it into two discs. Wrap each disc in plastic wrap or put them in individual freezer bags, and chill for 30 minutes before use, or freeze the dough for up to 1 month, thawing for 2 hours in the refrigerator before using.

TIP *If you don't have the time or inclination to make your own pie dough, Whole Foods and Trader Joe's both make good ready-to-use piecrusts. Pillsbury's crusts work well, too.*

Kentucky Bourbon Pecan Pie
WITH CHOCOLATE IN A PRETZEL CRUST

Makes one 10-inch pie

We added semisweet chocolate chips, a good splash of Woodford Reserve bourbon, and a pretzel crust (though you can use our Classic Piecrust, facing page, instead) to our traditional pecan pie. Sweet and a little salty, with a boozy backbone and a savory undertone, each bite hits almost every part of the palate at once.

This is a mix-and-pour recipe, so it's quick to pull off during high-stress holidays and you can wow your guests without a lot of work. We often make it for tailgating at Twilight Polo or the Virginia Gold Cup steeplechase (because, well, *bourbon*).

CRUST:

1½ cups crushed salted pretzels (about 4 cups traditional or stick pretzels)

¼ cup (1 stick) unsalted butter, melted and slightly cooled

¼ cup packed dark brown sugar

FILLING:

½ cup granulated sugar

¼ cup sorghum syrup

¼ cup light corn syrup

1 large egg

1 tablespoon bourbon

2 tablespoons unsalted butter, melted

Pinch of ground cinnamon

Pinch of kosher salt

1½ cups pecan halves

½ cup semisweet chocolate chips

Smoked sugar (I like Bourbon Barrel Foods) or turbinado sugar, for sprinkling

1. **Make the crust:** In a large bowl, mix the pretzels, melted butter, and brown sugar until well combined. Press evenly into the bottom and sides of a 10-inch pie pan. Refrigerate for 20 minutes.

2. Preheat the oven to 325°F. Place a raised wire rack inside a rimmed baking sheet.

3. **Make the filling:** In a medium bowl, whisk together the granulated sugar, sorghum syrup, corn syrup, egg, bourbon, melted butter, cinnamon, and salt until well mixed. Don't overwhip; you don't want the mixture to get thick and foamy.

4. Evenly spread the pecans and the chocolate chips over the chilled crust. Pour in the sugar-egg mixture, making sure all the pecans are coated. Sprinkle with a small handful of smoked sugar.

5. Carefully place the pie on the prepared baking sheet. Bake for 30 minutes, turning the baking sheet after 15 minutes, until the top is a rich brown. Give the pan a shake in the oven; if the filling seems too jiggly, bake for a few more minutes until all but the center inch or so is totally firm. Let cool on a raised wire rack.

MEET OUR
PRODUCERS
Bourbon
Barrel Foods
PAGE 214

TIP *When baking pies, we like to set the pie pan on a raised wire rack set on a baking sheet. It gets more heat circulating underneath the pan, ensuring that the bottom crust bakes completely.*

RED TRUCK BAKERY COOKBOOK

Strawberry Rhubarb Pie

Makes one 10-inch pie

My dad was a dessert purist who loved straight-up rhubarb pie, but it was always too one-note and tart for my liking. To sweeten it and incorporate a lightly floral component, I added strawberries brightened with lemon zest, cinnamon, and ginger. They're the perfect counterpoint.

Dad would probably frown upon my version of the pie, but our customers like it this way. Everyone loves seeing it appear on our shelves, if only because each year it marks the first fresh-fruit (or fresh-vegetable, in the case of rhubarb) pie after a long winter.

3 or 4 stalks fresh rhubarb, sliced on an angle into ¼-inch-wide pieces (2½ cups)

4 cups fresh strawberries (about 2 pints), hulled, halved if large

1¼ cups sugar

½ cup cornstarch

¼ teaspoon ground cinnamon

⅛ teaspoon ground or freshly grated nutmeg

⅛ teaspoon ground ginger

1 teaspoon lemon zest

2 teaspoons fresh lemon juice

1 recipe Classic Piecrust dough (page 60), or 2 store-bought crusts

2 tablespoons unsalted butter, chilled and cubed

1 large egg, whisked with 1 tablespoon water

Vanilla ice cream, for serving (optional)

1. Preheat the oven to 375°F. Place a raised wire rack inside a rimmed baking sheet.

2. In a large bowl, combine the rhubarb and the strawberries.

3. In a medium bowl, mix together the sugar, cornstarch, cinnamon, nutmeg, ginger, and lemon zest. Add the sugar mixture to the rhubarb and strawberries and toss to combine. Stir in the lemon juice. Let sit for a few minutes to allow the fruit to release juices.

4. Roll out one disc of pie dough into a 13-inch round and fit it into a 10-inch pie pan, leaving the crust overhanging. Pour the strawberry-rhubarb mixture into the crust and dot the top of the fruit with butter.

5. Roll out the second disc of dough into a roughly 18 x 13-inch rectangle. Cut it crosswise into six 3 x 13-inch strips.

6. Create a lattice crust by laying three strips of dough across the pie horizontally, then laying three strips of dough perpendicularly across them. Weave the top strips of dough over and under those on the bottom. Trim the dough about 2 inches from the pan, and roll and crimp the edges, combining the lattice crust with the dough in the pan. Brush the dough with egg wash.

7. Carefully place the pie on the prepared baking sheet. Bake for 90 minutes, turning after each 30 minutes or until the center is bubbling. Let cool on a raised wire rack.

8. Serve with vanilla ice cream, if desired.

Harvest Apple Pie

Makes one 10-inch pie

Both bakery locations are on the edge of the Shenandoah Valley, so we're at the core of apple country. Our local orchards provide enough apples for us to make pies throughout the fall and winter, and if we're lucky, they'll even have enough stored away to get us through until spring. For this recipe, I like using Honeycrisp, Mutsu, or Golden Delicious apples, though Granny Smiths will always suffice. When shopping for apples, beware of leathery, weathered skin, which means the apples are old or have been refrigerated for a long period. The apple's flavor will be diminished and the texture will be off—not pie-worthy.

When it comes to savoring a slice, I remember my dad's favorite line, "Apple pie without some cheese is like a kiss without a squeeze." He always had a good-sized hunk of Cheddar on his plate.

1 recipe Classic Piecrust dough (page 60), or 2 store-bought crusts

1¼ cups sugar

1½ teaspoons orange zest

½ cup cornstarch

¼ teaspoon ground cinnamon

⅛ teaspoon ground or freshly grated nutmeg

8 cups sliced peeled apples (from 6 to 8 apples)

½ cup walnut pieces

½ cup dried cherries or cranberries

2 tablespoons unsalted butter, chilled and cubed

1 large egg, whisked with 1 tablespoon water

Cheese, for serving (optional)

1. Preheat the oven to 325°F. Place a raised wire rack inside a rimmed baking sheet.

2. In a small bowl, combine the sugar and the orange zest. Let sit for a few minutes to allow the orange flavor to infuse the sugar. Add the cornstarch, cinnamon, and nutmeg. Put the apples in a large bowl, pour the sugar mixture on top, and toss to combine.

3. Roll out one disc of pie dough into a 13-inch round, fit it into a 10-inch pie pan, and trim the edges. Fill the pie shell with the apple mixture. Evenly spread the walnut pieces and the dried cherries on top; fold them carefully into the apples. Scatter the butter on top.

4. Roll out the second disc of dough and set it over the filling. Trim and crimp the edges, sealing in the filling. Cut a few slits in the top. Brush with the egg wash.

5. Carefully place the pie on the prepared baking sheet and bake for 1 hour, turning the baking sheet halfway through, until the pie filling is bubbling through the top slits. Let cool on a raised wire rack for 30 minutes.

6. Serve with cheese (I like a sharp, aged Cheddar), if desired.

RED TRUCK BAKERY COOKBOOK

Black and Blueberry Pie
WITH CORNMEAL CRUST

Makes one 10-inch pie

At our farm, blueberries ripen in late June on three huge bushes that must be eighty years old; nearby blackberries soon follow. This pie celebrates that sweet seasonal overlap. It's served in a cornmeal crust to reinforce the summery sensibility and earthy sweetness. Fuss-free and full of flavor, a slice pairs well with a scoop of vanilla ice cream or a tall glass of cold milk—or both, if you're feeling indulgent.

CORNMEAL CRUST:

½ cup unbleached all-purpose flour, sifted, plus more for dusting

½ cup cornmeal

2 teaspoons lemon zest

¼ cup granulated sugar

½ teaspoon kosher salt

4 tablespoons (½ stick) unsalted butter, chilled and cubed

2 tablespoons vegetable shortening, chilled

1 large egg yolk

1 tablespoon plus 2 teaspoons ice water, plus more as needed

FILLING:

¾ cup granulated sugar

¼ cup plus 2 tablespoons cornstarch

1 teaspoon chopped crystallized ginger, or a pinch of ground ginger

2 pinches of kosher salt

½ teaspoon lemon zest

3 cups fresh blueberries

2 cups fresh blackberries

STREUSEL:

1¼ cups unbleached all-purpose flour, sifted

½ cup packed light brown sugar

½ cup (1 stick) unsalted butter, chilled and cubed

1 teaspoon ground ginger

2 tablespoons unsalted butter, chilled and chopped into 6 pieces

1. Make the crust: In a food processor, combine the flour, cornmeal, lemon zest, granulated sugar, and salt. Gently pulse a few times. Add the butter and shortening and pulse until pea-sized lumps form.

2. In a small bowl, whisk together the egg yolk and the ice water. Drizzle the egg mixture into the flour mixture and process just until the dough holds together. Add a bit more ice water, 1 teaspoon at a time, if needed.

3. Turn the dough out onto a lightly floured surface. Pull the dough together into a pile and knead it a few times until clumped. Form it into a disc about 1 inch thick. Place the disc between two pieces of parchment paper and refrigerate for at least 1 hour.

4. Meanwhile, make the filling: In a large bowl, mix together the granulated sugar, cornstarch, ginger, salt, and lemon zest. Add the blueberries and blackberries and gently mix with your fingers, reaching under the fruit to pull up the sugar mixture and evenly distribute it over the fruit. Set aside for 10 minutes, allowing the sugar to pull a bit of juice from the berries.

(recipe continues)

5. **Make the streusel:** In the bowl of a stand mixer fitted with the paddle attachment, combine the flour, brown sugar, butter, and ginger and beat on medium speed until pea-sized lumps form. Do not overmix; if it reaches a paste-like consistency, it will be unusable.

6. Preheat the oven to 375°F. Place a raised wire rack inside a rimmed baking sheet.

7. Remove the pie dough from the refrigerator 15 minutes before you plan on working with it. Roll out the dough into a 13-inch round, fit it into a 10-inch pie pan, trim, and crimp the edges.

8. Add the berry filling. Scatter the butter pieces on top, followed by streusel topping.

9. Carefully place the pie on the prepared baking sheet. Bake for 1 hour, turning the baking sheet halfway through, until the pie filling is bubbling out from under the streusel topping. Let cool completely on a raised wire rack.

Funeral Pie
(Raisin Pie)

Makes one 10-inch pie

I cherish my grandmother's dark wood recipe box that sits in the kitchen of my farmhouse. Flipping through the 3 x 5-inch index cards covered with beautiful cursive—a by-product of her years as an English teacher in a one-room schoolhouse—her recipe for Funeral Pie made with raisins soaked in pineapple juice jumped out at me. Curious about its origins, I asked a relative. She said it was a very traditional Southern offering for a family after a loss, and that my grandmother made a pretty tasty version.

Her notes on the card mention to "cut out decorated shapes from pastry & arrange on top." I like the idea of using shapes, because it livens up the pie, especially on a sad occasion.

Before you can begin, you'll need to soak the raisins in pineapple juice for several hours to plump them.

3 cups raisins

1¾ cups pineapple juice

1 recipe Classic Piecrust dough (page 60), or 2 store-bought crusts

¼ cup plus 2 tablespoons cornstarch

¾ cup packed light brown sugar

⅛ teaspoon kosher salt

2 tablespoons fresh lemon juice

2 tablespoons unsalted butter, melted

1 large egg, whisked with 1 tablespoon water

1. Soak the raisins in the pineapple juice for at least 4 hours and up to 8 hours.

2. Roll out one disc of pie dough into a 13-inch round, fit it into a 10-inch pie pan, trim, and crimp the edges. Chill for 1 hour.

3. Roll out the second disc of dough to ¼-inch thickness and use a leaf-shaped cookie cutter—or another shape of your choosing—to cut out enough shapes to cover the top of the pie. Place the shapes on a parchment-lined baking sheet, spacing them 1 inch apart. Chill for 1 hour.

4. When the raisins have been soaked and you're ready to bake the pie, preheat the oven to 375°F. Place a raised wire rack inside a rimmed baking sheet.

5. In a large saucepan, whisk together the cornstarch, brown sugar, and salt. Drain the raisins, reserving ¼ cup of the pineapple juice, and add the raisins and reserved pineapple juice to the cornstarch mixture. Cook over medium heat, stirring continuously, for 20 to 25 minutes, until the liquid is deep brown and has reduced by at least half. Remove the pan from the heat and let the raisin mixture cool slightly. Stir in the lemon juice and melted butter.

6. Fill the chilled pie shell with the cooled raisin mixture. Top with the crust cutouts and lightly brush with the egg wash. Carefully place the pie on the prepared baking sheet. Bake for 30 minutes, turning the baking sheet after 15 minutes, until the filling is bubbling up at the center. Let cool completely on a raised wire rack before slicing and serving.

Sweet Potato Pecan Pie
(The Presidential Pie)

Makes one 10-inch pie

If a first-time visitor knows just one item from the bakery, it's probably this pie, which President Obama made famous. It's actually two pies in one: with a bottom layer of sweet potato filling topped off with a layer of bourbon filling and plenty of pecans, there's no surprise why it's a favorite from the West Wing to eastern Kentucky and many points beyond.

½ recipe Classic Piecrust dough (page 60), or 1 store-bought crust

SWEET POTATO FILLING:

1 cup cooked and mashed sweet potato flesh (from about 3 large sweet potatoes)

1 tablespoon unsalted butter, at room temperature

1 cup granulated sugar

¼ cup packed dark brown sugar

1 large egg, beaten

¼ teaspoon ground cinnamon

¼ teaspoon ground ginger

¼ teaspoon ground or freshly grated nutmeg

2 tablespoons heavy cream

1 tablespoon bourbon

BOURBON FILLING:

½ cup granulated sugar

2 large eggs, beaten

¼ cup sorghum syrup

¾ cup light corn syrup

1 tablespoon bourbon

2 tablespoons unsalted butter, melted

Pinch of ground cinnamon

Pinch of kosher salt

2 cups unsalted pecan halves

1. Roll out the pie dough into a 13-inch round, fit it into a 10-inch pie pan, trim, and crimp the edges. Chill for 1 hour.

2. Preheat the oven to 325°F. Place a raised wire rack inside a rimmed baking sheet.

3. **Make the sweet potato filling:** In the bowl of a stand mixer fitted with the whisk attachment, beat the sweet potato on medium speed until fluffy and smooth. Swap the whisk attachment for the paddle attachment and add the butter. Mix well to combine. Add the granulated sugar, brown sugar, egg, cinnamon, ginger, and nutmeg and beat on medium speed until creamy. Scrape down the sides. Add the cream and bourbon and mix on medium speed until thoroughly incorporated.

4. **Make the bourbon filling:** In a large bowl, whisk together the granulated sugar, eggs, sorghum syrup, corn syrup, bourbon, melted butter, cinnamon, and salt until thoroughly combined. Don't overbeat; you don't want the mixture to get thick and foamy.

5. Pour the sweet potato filling into the pie shell, filling it halfway (you may have some left over). Smooth evenly with a spatula or the back of a spoon.

6. Pour in half the bourbon filling, spreading it evenly. Scatter the pecans over the filling. Add the remaining bourbon filling on top of the pecans, using your fingers to make sure each pecan is coated.

7. Carefully place the pie on the prepared baking sheet. Bake for 1 hour 10 minutes, turning the baking sheet after 30 minutes. Give the pan a light shake; if the filling seems too liquid, bake for up to 20 minutes more, until the bourbon filling is firm. Let cool on a raised wire rack.

Bob and Buddy's Mincemeat Pie
WITH APPLE BRANDY

Makes one 10-inch pie

I named this pie after my mom's uncles, Bob Getz and Buddy Murray, co-owners of the Central Meat Market in Pacific Grove on the Monterey peninsula. *Esquire* magazine saluted our mincemeat pies a year or so after we first opened, mentioning my mission to resurrect "America's most perplexing dessert." The much-maligned pie often creates confusion with first-timers. It's not a savory meat pie, though it does contain suet—deliciously rich beef or mutton fat harvested from around the loins and kidneys. (You can buy suet at the butcher shop or the meat counter at any respectable grocery store, and high-quality Atora suet is available online.) Instead, the pie is packed with apples, raisins, warming spices, and a couple of jiggers of brandy to add sweetness and a mellow undertone. We use Mt. Defiance apple brandy from nearby Middleburg, Virginia, because it's sweeter and fruitier than most, but whatever you have on hand should do the trick.

The mincemeat filling requires four to five hours of resting before you can make this pie; it allows the raisins to soak up the liquids.

2½ cups finely chopped peeled Granny Smith apples (from about 3 medium apples)

½ cup golden raisins

½ cup dark raisins

½ cup dried currants

½ cup packed dark brown sugar

½ cup shredded beef suet

¼ cup apple brandy or brandy

2 teaspoons finely grated lemon zest

2 tablespoons fresh lemon juice

2 teaspoons finely grated orange zest

½ teaspoon ground allspice

½ teaspoon ground or freshly grated nutmeg

1 recipe Classic Piecrust dough (page 60), or 2 store-bought crusts

1 large egg, whisked with 1 tablespoon water

Smoked sugar (I like Bourbon Barrel Foods) or turbinado sugar, for sprinkling

1. In an airtight container, stir together the apples, golden raisins, dark raisins, currants, brown sugar, suet, brandy, lemon zest, lemon juice, orange zest, allspice, and nutmeg. Cover the container and chill for 8 to 9 hours, stirring occasionally.

2. Preheat the oven to 350°F. Place a raised wire rack inside a rimmed baking sheet.

3. Roll out one disc of the pie dough into a 13-inch round, fit it into a 10-inch pie pan, and trim the edges. Fill the pie shell with the mincemeat mixture.

4. Roll out the second disc of pie dough, drape it over the filling, trim, and crimp the edges. Cut a few slits in the top, then brush with the egg wash and sprinkle with smoked sugar.

5. Carefully place the pie on the prepared baking sheet. Bake for 1 hour, turning the baking sheet after 20 minutes, until the crust is golden and the filling is bubbling out of the center slits. Let cool completely on a raised wire rack before slicing and serving.

Pawpaw Chess Pie

Makes one 10-inch pie

I enjoy resurrecting antique Appalachian ingredients that have fallen out of favor over the years. Pawpaws are a native wild fruit prevalent in the mid-Atlantic with a tropical-ish taste, something akin to bananas mixed with apples, pears, and a touch of mango. Our buddy Tarver King, a James Beard–nominated chef at the Restaurant at Patowmack Farm in Lovettsville, Virginia, loves foraging for offbeat ingredients, and he let me in on a few secret locations where pawpaws grow. You don't need to go tramping through the woods to make this recipe, though; you can buy them at many farmer's markets from early September through late October, or purchase frozen pawpaw puree online anytime.

GRAHAM CRACKER CRUST:

1½ cups graham cracker crumbs (12 graham crackers)

5 tablespoons unsalted butter, melted and cooled slightly

½ cup shredded coconut, toasted

¼ cup sugar

Pinch of kosher salt

Pinch of ground cinnamon

FILLING:

¾ cup sugar

¼ cup cornstarch

3 large egg yolks, lightly beaten

1½ cups buttermilk

½ cup heavy cream

1 cup pureed pawpaw pulp

1. **Make the crust:** In a medium bowl, mix the graham cracker crumbs, melted butter, coconut, sugar, salt, and cinnamon until combined. Press evenly into the bottom and sides of a 10-inch pie pan. Chill for 1 hour.

2. Preheat the oven to 350°F. Place a raised wire rack inside a rimmed baking sheet.

3. **Make the filling:** In a large saucepan, combine the sugar and cornstarch. Add the egg yolks, buttermilk, and cream. Stir to mix well, then add the pawpaw pulp. Cook over low heat, stirring continuously, for 8 to 10 minutes, until it has the consistency of thick applesauce. Remove the pan from the heat and let cool.

4. Pour the pawpaw mixture into the chilled crust to just below the edge of the pie pan. Carefully place the pie on the prepared baking sheet. Bake for 20 to 30 minutes, until slightly browned at the center—start checking at the 20-minute mark. Let cool completely before cutting.

TIP *Use a second pie pan to evenly press the graham cracker crust.*

Watermelon Pie

Makes one 10-inch pie

I was visiting Knoxville, Tennessee, for a food writer's conference in 2017, which included a dinner at J.C. Holdway restaurant, a reviver of southeastern regional cuisine. When James Beard award–winning chef Joseph Lenn came out to tell us the menu for the evening, those of us in the back of the noisy dining room mistakenly heard watermelon pie would be served for dessert. What eventually arrived was buttermilk pie, but I was intrigued by the former and went to work on a recipe. Watermelon is a tough flavor to capture, but the whipped cream and condensed milk here carry it nicely. A cool slice of this pie is just as refreshing as a wedge of watermelon on a sweltering summer day.

Note that this pie requires chilling eight hours before serving.

GRAHAM CRACKER CRUST:

2 teaspoons lime zest

¼ cup sugar

1½ cups graham cracker crumbs (from 12 graham crackers)

5 tablespoons unsalted butter, melted and cooled slightly

Pinch of kosher salt

FILLING:

1 cup heavy cream

1 (14-ounce) can sweetened condensed milk

¼ cup fresh lime juice

2 cups chopped watermelon, seeded, very well drained, and pureed

1 tablespoon finely chopped fresh mint

2 teaspoons finely chopped fresh basil

1. Preheat the oven to 375°F.

2. Make the crust: In a small bowl, combine the lime zest and the sugar. Let sit for a few minutes to allow the lime flavor to infuse the sugar.

3. In a large bowl, mix together the lime-sugar mixture, graham cracker crumbs, melted butter, and salt. Press the crust into the bottom and sides of a 10-inch pie pan.

4. Bake for 7 minutes. Remove from the oven and let cool.

5. Make the filling: In the bowl of a stand mixer fitted with the whisk attachment, whip the cream until it holds firm peaks.

6. In a large bowl, mix together the condensed milk and the lime juice until thickened. Using a spatula, gently fold in the whipped cream until well combined. Fold in the watermelon puree, mint, and basil until well combined.

7. Spoon the filling into the crust and smooth the top with a spatula or the back of a spoon.

8. Chill for at least 8 hours or up to overnight before slicing and serving.

RED TRUCK BAKERY COOKBOOK

Apricot and Plum Hand Pies

Makes 12 to 15 hand pies

Sometimes you want pie on the go, but a slice isn't convenient to eat. That's why I like these portable pastries, which you can enjoy with one hand while the other stays on the wheel. You can put nearly any fruit inside (apple works really well), but I like pocketing them with a custardy-coated mix of sweet apricots and lush plums.

1 cup heavy cream

½ cup granulated sugar

¼ teaspoon kosher salt

1 teaspoon lemon zest

1 large egg

1 large egg yolk

2 tablespoons cornstarch

2 tablespoons unsalted butter

¼ teaspoon pure vanilla extract

1 cup diced plums (about 2 plums)

1 cup diced fresh apricots (about 2 apricots)

2 recipes Classic Piecrust dough (page 60), or 4 store-bought crusts

1 large egg, whisked with 1 tablespoon water

Turbinado sugar, for sprinkling

1. Preheat the oven to 375°F. Line a baking sheet with parchment paper.

2. In a medium saucepan, combine the cream, ¼ cup of the granulated sugar, the salt, and the lemon zest and bring to a low boil over medium heat.

3. In a small bowl, whisk together the egg, egg yolk, remaining ¼ cup granulated sugar, and the cornstarch. Add to the saucepan and whisk for 1 minute.

4. Remove the pan from the heat and whisk in the butter and vanilla. Mix in the fruit until thoroughly combined.

5. Roll out all four discs of pie dough to a thickness of ¼ inch and cut them into twelve to fifteen 6-inch rounds (use an inverted bowl as a guide). Brush the edge of half of each round with the egg wash. Place roughly 2 tablespoons of the fruit mixture in the middle of the half that's been egg washed. Fold over the other side and press the edges with the tines of a fork to seal. Pierce the tops of the hand pies once with the tines of a fork. Brush with the egg wash and sprinkle liberally with turbinado sugar.

6. Transfer the hand pies to the prepared baking sheet and bake for 30 minutes, turning the baking sheet after 15 minutes, until the crusts are golden brown. Transfer the hand pies to a raised wire rack to cool.

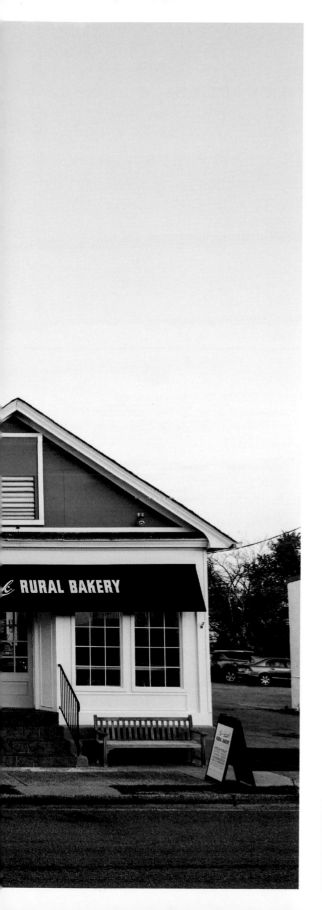

Quiche, Casseroles, and Savory Pies

Virginia Country Ham
AND GRUYÈRE QUICHE

Makes one 9-inch quiche

This comforting dish is a crowd-pleaser. Dotted with classic Virginia country ham, which is salt-cured and aged on the dry side, it gives visitors a real taste of the South. For more than fifty years, Tom and his family at Calhoun's Country Hams in nearby Culpeper County have been crafting what I consider to be the best country ham around. The pork hinds start off in well-spiced brine, so they boast a rich flavor, but they aren't packed full of preservatives and excess sodium. Calhoun's ships nationwide, if you want to replicate our recipe exactly to enjoy how well country ham pairs with the nuttiness of the Gruyère.

½ recipe Savory Pie and Quiche Crust dough (page 102), or 1 store-bought crust

1 tablespoon Dijon mustard

1 tablespoon olive oil

1 medium yellow onion, cut into medium dice

Kosher salt and freshly ground black pepper

2 large eggs

1 cup half-and-half

¼ teaspoon ground or freshly grated nutmeg

1½ cups grated Gruyère cheese

1 cup coarsely chopped Virginia country ham

1 cup coarsely chopped Black Forest ham or other smoked cooked ham

3 scallions, thinly sliced

1. Roll out the pie dough to a round 11 inches in diameter. Gently pick up the dough without stretching it and lay it in a 9-inch fluted metal or ceramic quiche pan, letting the sides of the round droop over the pan edge while tucking the dough with your fingers against the bottom of the pan. Fold the overhang back over the edge toward the inside of the pan, squeezing it together as you turn the pan to give the top of the crust a bit more thickness. If using a fluted metal pan, run your rolling pin over the pan, pressing to trim the dough against the top edge of the pan, and remove the excess dough.

2. Brush the bottom of the crust with the mustard. Chill until ready to use.

3. Preheat the oven to 375°F. Place a raised wire rack inside a rimmed baking sheet.

4. In a medium skillet, heat the olive oil over medium heat. When the oil is shimmering, lower the heat and add the onion and season with salt and pepper. Cook slowly, stirring frequently, until golden. Remove the pan from the heat and set aside to cool.

5. In a large bowl, whisk together the eggs and half-and-half. Add ¼ teaspoon salt, ¼ teaspoon pepper, and the nutmeg and whisk again to combine.

6. Place the chilled crust on the prepared baking sheet. Spread the cooled onions evenly over the bottom. Evenly spread half the Gruyère and the Virginia country ham, Black Forest ham, and scallions over the onions. Finish with the remaining cheese. Whisk the egg mixture one last time to distribute the spices and pour it into the crust to about ¼ inch below the edge.

7. Bake for 30 to 40 minutes, turning the baking sheet after 20 minutes, until the egg mixture is set and the crust is golden brown. Let cool completely before slicing and serving.

Appalachian Pie
WITH RAMPS AND MORELS

Makes one 9-inch pie

This breakfast pie celebrates the springtime bounty of Appalachia by showcasing wild ramps and morel mushrooms. The former are slender onions with green fronds and a garlicky aroma. They taste similar to leeks, but with more astringency, making them a perfect complement to rich morel mushrooms. Foragers in the area command a premium for both ingredients, which makes this pie quite luxe (using fresh local eggs further improves the quality). The ingredients can often be found at farmer's markets in the mid-Atlantic and beyond, usually starting in April and going into June. If they're not native to your region, you can order them online from websites such as Earthy.com.

½ recipe Savory Pie and Quiche Crust dough (page 102), or 1 store-bought crust

1 tablespoon plus 2 teaspoons Dijon mustard

1 tablespoon olive oil

24 ramps, sliced 1 inch thick

3 large eggs

1 cup half-and-half

¼ teaspoon kosher salt

¼ teaspoon freshly ground black pepper

¼ teaspoon ground or freshly grated nutmeg

1½ cups grated Gruyère cheese

2 cups roughly chopped morel mushrooms

1. Roll out the pie dough to a round 11 inches in diameter. Gently pick up the round without stretching it and lay it in a 9-inch fluted metal or ceramic quiche pan, letting the sides of the round droop over the pan edge while tucking the dough with your fingers against the bottom of the pan. Fold the overhang back over the edge toward the inside of the pan, squeezing it together as you turn the pan to give the top of the crust a bit more thickness. If using a fluted metal pan, run your rolling pin over the pan, pressing to trim the dough against the top edge of the pan, and remove the excess dough.

2. Brush the bottom of the crust with the mustard. Chill until ready to use.

3. Preheat the oven to 375°F. Place a raised wire rack inside a rimmed baking sheet.

4. In a large skillet, heat the olive oil over medium heat. When the oil is shimmering, add the ramps and cook, stirring frequently, until golden, about 5 minutes. Remove the pan from the heat and let cool.

5. In a medium bowl, whisk together the eggs and half-and-half. Add the salt, pepper, and nutmeg and mix until combined.

6. Place the chilled crust on the prepared baking sheet. Evenly spread the ramps over the bottom of the crust. Sprinkle half the cheese over the ramps, followed by all the morels. Sprinkle with the remaining cheese. Pour in the egg mixture, filling the crust to about ¼ inch below the edge.

7. Bake for 50 minutes, turning the baking sheet after 30 minutes, until the top of the egg mixture is golden brown. Let cool slightly before slicing and serving.

Spoonbread
WITH FIGS AND MASCARPONE

Serves 6 to 8

This recipe is not for a bread, but rather for a traditional Southern side dish similar to a savory soufflé. Usually it's made solely with cornmeal; however, I also add some larger grits—I appreciate their coarser texture—and incorporate a touch of honey and fresh figs to lend a subtle sweetness. Think about making a batch for your Thanksgiving spread; it'll be the sleeper hit of the feast.

5 tablespoons unsalted butter, plus more for greasing

1 cup cornmeal

½ cup uncooked grits (not instant)

1 cup heavy cream

1 cup mascarpone cheese

½ cup grated pecorino cheese

3 tablespoons honey

¼ teaspoon lemon zest

1 teaspoon kosher salt

3 large eggs, separated

6 ripe figs, quartered

1. Preheat the oven to 375°F. Generously grease a 9-inch square cake pan with butter.

2. In a medium pot, combine the cornmeal, grits, and 2½ cups water. Cook over low heat, stirring frequently, for 30 minutes, until very thick and smooth.

3. Remove the pot from the heat and whisk in the butter, cream, mascarpone, pecorino, honey, and lemon zest until thoroughly combined. Add the salt, then whisk in the egg yolks.

4. In the bowl of a stand mixer fitted with the whisk attachment, whip the egg whites until they hold soft peaks. Using a spatula, carefully fold the whipped egg whites into the batter until incorporated.

5. Pour the batter into the prepared pan and dot it with the figs, pushing them into the batter until submerged with only their tops showing. Bake for 30 minutes, until golden brown and puffed up. Let cool for 10 minutes before serving.

Shrimp and Grits Pandowdy

Serves 6 to 8

I've long been intrigued by traditional Southern dishes, such as the pandowdy, a nineteenth-century dessert similar to a cobbler. As a Southern baker, I feel a bit of responsibility to keep these heritage recipes alive while putting my own spin on them. I crossed a traditional pandowdy with shrimp and grits, one of my all-time favorite Low Country classics, which I first tasted at Bill Neal's Crook's Corner in Chapel Hill, North Carolina. And instead of a crunchy crumb topping, we overlay balls of biscuit dough atop the filling to create a veritable patchwork quilt.

PANDOWDY BISCUITS:

1¾ cups unbleached all-purpose flour, sifted, plus more for dusting

2 teaspoons baking powder

¼ teaspoon baking soda

1 teaspoon kosher salt

1¼ teaspoons sugar

¼ cup vegetable shortening, at room temperature

¼ cup (½ stick) unsalted butter, chilled and cubed, plus 4 tablespoons (½ stick), at room temperature

½ cup buttermilk

¼ cup grated Cheddar cheese

2 tablespoons thinly sliced scallions

GRITS:

1 cup chicken broth

1 cup stone-ground grits

6 tablespoons (¾ stick) unsalted butter

1 teaspoon Tabasco, or to taste

1 teaspoon kosher salt

1 teaspoon freshly ground black pepper

1 cup grated Cheddar cheese

2 large tomatoes, chopped (about 2 cups)

SHRIMP:

4 applewood-smoked bacon slices, diced

2 cups sliced mushrooms

1 cup thinly sliced scallions (about 2 bunches)

2 garlic cloves, chopped

1 pound fresh shrimp, peeled and deveined, rinsed, and dried

2 teaspoons red pepper flakes, or to taste

1 tablespoon fresh lemon juice

1 tablespoon chopped fresh parsley

1. **Make the pandowdy biscuits:** In a large bowl, whisk together the flour, baking powder, baking soda, salt, and sugar. Cut the shortening and the chilled cubed butter into the flour mixture with your fingers, two knives, or a pastry blender (not a mixer) until broken down into pea-sized pieces. Pour the buttermilk into the dry mixture all at once and, using a wooden spoon, fold in the buttermilk as quickly and as gently as possible. Flour your hands and reach into the bowl and under the dough and combine, flipping it around. Mix it up as gently as possible without being too tough on the dough. The dough will be sticky, but manageable. Add the cheese and scallions and mix them into the dough without being too rough. Set aside.

2. **Make the grits:** In a large saucepan, bring 3 cups water to a boil over high heat. Add the broth. Add the grits by hand, letting them flow gradually through your fingers into the pot. Cook, stirring, until thick and blended, about 10 minutes. Add the butter, Tabasco, salt, and black pepper. Reduce the heat to low and simmer, stirring occasionally, for 10 minutes, or until thickened. Remove the pan from the heat and add the cheese and tomatoes.

(recipe continues)

RED TRUCK BAKERY COOKBOOK

3. **Make the shrimp:** In a large skillet, cook the bacon over medium heat until the edges start to brown, about 4 minutes (we like ours soft and not too well-done). Using a slotted spoon, transfer the bacon to a small bowl, reserving as much bacon grease in the pan as possible. Add the mushrooms, scallions, and garlic to the pan and cook, stirring, over medium heat until the mushrooms and garlic are golden brown, about 5 minutes. Add the shrimp and cook just until pink, about 2 minutes. Add the cooked bacon. Remove the pan from the heat and stir in the red pepper flakes, lemon juice, and parsley.

4. Preheat the oven to 350°F. Grease a 9-inch round casserole dish with butter.

5. Pour the cooked grits into the prepared casserole dish. Evenly spread the shrimp mixture over the top, stirring just enough to slightly mix it with the grits.

6. Add the pandowdy biscuit topping by dropping pinches of dough all over the shrimp and grits (it's okay if there are some small gaps). Bake for 30 minutes, until the topping is golden brown and puffed. Let cool slightly and serve warm.

Mac 'n' Pimento Cheese

Serves 6

We long pondered using Aunt Darla's Smoky Pimento Cheese (page 198) as the basis for a mac 'n' cheese. After a couple of experiments, we created this stovetop version that doesn't require any baking. Supremely creamy and rich with the flavors of the pimento cheese, it's darn indulgent. It's perfect for housewarming parties, barbecues, and to deliver to new moms and dads, who might need some serious comfort food to combat the stress and fatigue of parenthood.

Kosher salt

1 pound dried elbow macaroni

3 tablespoons unsalted butter

2 tablespoons unbleached all-purpose flour

3 cups whole milk

2 cups Aunt Darla's Smoky Pimento Cheese (page 198, or use store-bought)

¾ cup grated Gruyère cheese

½ cup grated Parmesan cheese

½ cup chopped scallions (about 6 scallions)

⅛ teaspoon cayenne pepper

⅛ teaspoon smoked paprika

Pinch of freshly ground white pepper

Freshly ground black pepper

1. Bring large pot of salted water to a boil over high heat. Add the pasta and cook according to the package instructions. Drain in a colander, rinse with cold water, and set aside.

2. In the same pot, melt the butter over medium heat. Whisk in the flour and cook until bubbling, about 4 minutes. Add the milk, whisking to combine. Bring to a boil, whisking continuously to prevent scorching. Reduce the heat to medium-low and simmer, stirring occasionally, for 25 minutes, until the mixture has thickened.

3. Add the pimento, Gruyère, and Parmesan cheeses and stir until completely melted and smooth. Add the scallions, cayenne, paprika, and white pepper. Season with salt and black pepper. Add the pasta (reheat it briefly) and mix thoroughly to coat with the sauce. Serve immediately.

Chicken Potpie

Makes four 6-inch potpies

This dish, with juicy chunks of chicken, carrots, and peas swimming in thickened gravy, reminds me of the chicken potpies my mother served when I was growing up. There's something so comforting about these plump personal pies that it's no surprise they're among the top sellers at the bakery all year round (we offer them prebaked as well as unbaked and frozen). I keep an eye out for other versions of chicken potpies when traveling, and if they don't have a bottom crust, I pass them up—this filling begs to be completely wrapped in golden, buttery pastry.

Lucky for you, they're relatively easy to replicate at home. One critical step to remember is piercing the top crust with a knife or punching out a shape in the center in order to vent the pie. Forget that and the pie's contents will blow out the sides, creating a mess in the oven you won't soon forget.

You will need four 6-inch round pie pans; ovenproof bowls or disposable aluminum foil pans will work as well.

CHICKEN:

6 large boneless, skinless chicken breasts (about 2½ pounds)

2 tablespoons extra-virgin olive oil

Kosher salt and freshly ground black pepper

1 tablespoon finely chopped fresh rosemary

FILLING:

¾ cup (1½ sticks) unsalted butter

3 cups chopped yellow onions (about 3 medium)

¾ cup unbleached all-purpose flour, sifted

4 cups chicken broth

1 cup heavy cream

2 teaspoons kosher salt

1 teaspoon freshly ground black pepper

2 cups chopped carrots

1 (10-ounce) package frozen green peas

½ cup finely chopped fresh parsley

2 recipes Savory Pie and Quiche Crust dough (page 102), or 4 store-bought crusts

1 large egg, whisked with 1 tablespoon water

Sea salt and coarsely ground black pepper

1. Preheat the oven to 450°F.

2. Make the chicken: Rub the chicken breasts with the olive oil and sprinkle with salt, pepper, and the rosemary. Arrange on a rimmed baking sheet and bake for 15 to 20 minutes, until just cooked through. Let cool, then coarsely chop into large pieces.

3. Make the filling: In a large saucepan, melt the butter over medium-low heat. Add the onions and cook, stirring, for 15 minutes, until translucent. Add the flour and whisk continuously for a couple of minutes; you'll have a thick roux that will brown a little bit while you continue to whisk (but don't let it burn). While whisking, gradually add the broth. Make sure the mixture is blended completely and that none is stuck to the sides of the pot. Reduce the heat to low and add the cream, salt, and pepper. Whisk for another minute or so, remove the pot from the heat, and, using a wooden spoon or spatula, stir in the carrots, peas, parsley, and chopped chicken. Let cool.

(recipe continues)

4. Roll out all four discs of dough and cut them into four 9-inch rounds and four 7½-inch rounds (use inverted bowls as guides). Without stretching the dough, gently drape each larger dough round into an individual 6-inch pie pan about 2 inches deep, letting the round drape over the sides of the pan.

5. Divide the cooled chicken mixture among the four pie shells. Brush the rim of the dough with the egg wash, then set a smaller round of dough atop each and seal the edges of the bottom and top crusts together with your fingers. Trim the dough to about ½ inch around the outside edge of the pans. Roll the outside edges toward the top of the pans, just inside the rim, and crimp with your fingers or a fork.

6. Brush the top crusts with the egg wash and cut a couple of slits in the center of each. Sprinkle with sea salt and coarse black pepper.

7. At this point you can proceed with baking, or freeze and bake later. If freezing, wrap each pie tightly in plastic wrap and place in plastic freezer bags, freezing for up to 3 months.

8. Put the pans on a baking sheet and bake for 1 hour, turning the baking sheet after 30 minutes, until the mixture is bubbling out of the slits and the crusts are golden. Let cool slightly and serve.

9. If baking previously frozen potpies, let thaw for 20 minutes. Bake for 1 hour 15 minutes on a baking sheet, rotating halfway through, until the mixture is bubbling out of the slits and the crusts are golden.

SOUTH-BY-SOUTHWESTERN
Crab Deepdish

Serves 6

Even though we're out in Virginia's Piedmont region, we're still in Chesapeake Bay country. There is no dish more sacred here than crab cakes made with blue crabs. We've transformed them into a casserole—I call it a deepdish—with a Southwestern accent by incorporating fresh cilantro, zippy jalapeño, and toasted cornbread.

Every October, we drive over to The Plains, Virginia, with picnic hampers brimming with brunch fare to watch the Virginia Gold Cup steeplechase. This casserole is always a big hit with our friends, who come by the tailgate party we throw out of the back of our red truck. They invariably ask to "just try a bite." The next thing we know, they're fixing up a plate, and they've joined our party.

This recipe works best in a 2-quart glass casserole dish with a lid.

Nonstick cooking spray

1 cup Jalapeño Mayonnaise (recipe follows), plus more for serving

3 large eggs

2 cups half-and-half

1 teaspoon mustard powder

1 teaspoon sea salt

½ teaspoon freshly ground black pepper

1 teaspoon red pepper flakes

1 cup canned or fresh corn kernels

½ cup finely diced green bell pepper (about ½ pepper)

3 tablespoons finely diced red onion (about ¼ medium onion)

1 cup shredded pepper Jack cheese

1 cup shredded Parmesan cheese

2 cups crumbled cornbread

1 pound canned or fresh lump crabmeat

1. Preheat the oven to 325°F. Coat a 2-quart casserole dish and its lid with nonstick spray.

2. In a large bowl, whisk together the jalapeño mayonnaise, eggs, half-and-half, mustard powder, salt, black pepper, and red pepper flakes until combined. Stir in the corn, bell pepper, onion, pepper Jack, half of the Parmesan, and the cornbread. Add the crab and mix well. Transfer the batter to the prepared casserole dish and sprinkle with the remaining Parmesan.

3. Bake, uncovered, for 30 minutes. Cover with the lid and bake for 30 to 40 minutes more, until a knife inserted into the center of the casserole comes out clean.

4. Serve warm, with more jalapeño mayonnaise alongside as a condiment.

Jalapeño Mayonnaise
Makes 2½ cups

3 tablespoons diced red onion (about ¼ medium onion)

¼ cup coarsely chopped fresh cilantro

1½ medium jalapeños, seeded

2 cups mayonnaise

2 teaspoons mustard powder

In a food processor, combine the onion, cilantro, and jalapeños. Process until finely chopped. Add the mayonnaise and mustard powder and process until smooth. Use immediately or refrigerate in an airtight container for up to 1 week. Any leftovers work great slathered on a sandwich or tacos.

RED TRUCK BAKERY COOKBOOK

New Year's Tamales

Makes about 24 tamales

I couldn't write a cookbook without including black-eyed peas and collard greens, especially since Dwight's aunt Edna had taught me to make her secret collard recipe. I've been enamored with the idea of making tamales for New Year's, and since black-eyed peas and collard greens are also used to ring in the New Year with health and wealth, I rolled the two traditions into one. Make a party out of it—get your guests involved when it comes time to stuff the cornhusks.

Masa harina and dried cornhusks are available at Latin supermarkets, many grocery stores, and online.

About 30 dried cornhusks

FILLING:

1 tablespoon canola oil

1 cup chopped pork shoulder or ham

1 cup chopped scallions (about 2 bunches)

2 garlic cloves, minced

4 thick-sliced smoked bacon slices, coarsely chopped

1 teaspoon kosher salt

½ teaspoon freshly ground black pepper

2 tablespoons roasted or sautéed diced green chiles, fresh or canned and drained

½ cup chicken broth

1 tablespoon chopped fresh parsley

½ teaspoon ground cumin

4 cups chopped collard greens and stems (about ½ pound)

1 (15-ounce) can black-eyed peas, rinsed and drained

2 tablespoons hot pepper vinegar (or brine from a jar of pickled jalapeños), or to taste

MASA:

1¾ cups plus 2 tablespoons masa harina

1 cup plus 2 tablespoons chicken broth

9 tablespoons unsalted butter, at room temperature

1½ teaspoons baking powder

1½ teaspoons kosher salt

1½ teaspoons smoked paprika

1½ cups fresh or thawed frozen corn

3 cups shredded pepper Jack cheese

Jezebel Sauce (page 204) or Comeback Sauce (page 205), for serving

1. Put the cornhusks in a large bowl, add hot water to cover, and soak for 20 minutes.

2. Meanwhile, make the filling: In a large pot, heat the canola oil over medium heat. When the oil is shimmering, add the pork shoulder and cook, turning, until browned on all sides, about 6 minutes. Add the scallions, garlic, and bacon and cook for 5 minutes, stirring continuously, until the bacon is cooked well but not dark. Add the salt, black pepper, and green chiles. Cook, stirring continuously, for 3 minutes, until the chiles start to soften. Stir in the broth, parsley, and cumin, and finally add the chopped collards. Reduce the heat to medium-low and cook, stirring frequently, for 25 minutes. Stir in the drained black-eyed peas. Add the vinegar. Remove the pot from the heat and let cool.

3. Make the masa: In a large bowl, mix together the masa harina and the broth with your hands or a wooden spoon. It will be a little crumbly.

4. In a separate large bowl, mix together the butter, baking powder, salt, and paprika until creamed.

(recipe continues)

RED TRUCK BAKERY COOKBOOK

5. Dry sauté the corn in a medium skillet until browned at the edges, stirring frequently, about 10 minutes.

6. Add the corn and cheese to the butter mixture and combine well. Add the masa and combine well. Divide the masa mixture into 3-tablespoon balls and form each ball into a log roughly the size of a Twix bar.

7. To create the tamales, place a log of masa lengthwise down the center of a soaked corn husk, about 2 inches from either short end. Flatten the masa with your hand into a thin rectangle. Spoon 2 to 3 tablespoons of the black-eyed pea mixture at the center of the masa in a straight line, stopping 1 inch from the top and bottom of the rectangle. Roll the long sides of the corn husk together so the masa mixture encases the black-eyed pea mixture. Roll the long sides of the husk toward the center until the filling is completely covered and tie the

top and bottom with kitchen twine or strips of soaked cornhusk.

8. Set a steamer basket or colander over a large pot filled with 3 to 4 inches of boiling water, making sure the water does not touch the bottom of the steamer. Lay the tamales in the steamer. It's okay to stack them to make them all fit. Steam over medium-low heat for 30 minutes, adding more water as needed so the pot doesn't boil dry.

9. Unwrap the tamales, discarding the husks (don't eat them!), and enjoy while still warm. Serve with Jezebel Sauce or Comeback Sauce as an accompaniment.

Jamie's Corn Pudding

Serves 6 to 8

Before I had a storefront, I was selling breads, pastries, and granola out of the back of my red truck. Jeff and Jamie Hedges live down the road from one of the country stores where I used to park, and they were among the first to stop by and stock up. Jamie is quite the cook herself; I love the fluffy corn pudding she served at parties. If she didn't make it, she'd get an earful from guests— starting with me.

I finally wrestled the recipe out of her, and I've added applewood-smoked bacon, fresh basil, and cherry tomatoes to reinforce the late-summer personality of this dish. Freshly harvested Silver Queen corn works best, I think, but any sweet corn will do, even a bag of frozen kernels from the grocery store (just make sure you drain it extremely well).

4 cups fresh or thawed frozen corn kernels

5 applewood-smoked bacon slices

1 cup quartered cherry tomatoes

4 fresh basil leaves, finely chopped, or 2 teaspoons dried basil

6 large eggs, gently stirred but not beaten

3 cups heavy cream

¼ cup sugar

1½ teaspoons kosher salt

1 tablespoon unbleached all-purpose flour

½ teaspoon baking powder

1. Pulse the corn in a food processor—six quick pulses should do the trick; you want the kernels to retain some of their body—then drain in a colander for at least 1 hour. Press on the corn to remove all the liquid and pat dry with paper towels, if needed, to ensure the corn is completely dry.

2. Meanwhile, preheat the oven to 325°F.

3. In a large skillet, cook the bacon over medium-low heat until done but not dark, about 10 minutes (we like ours soft and not too well-done), flipping occasionally to ensure even cooking. Transfer to a paper towel to drain and cool, then chop into small pieces.

4. Place the cherry tomatoes between paper towels and press gently to soak up any liquid.

5. In a 2-quart casserole dish, mix together the corn, bacon, tomatoes, basil, eggs, cream, sugar, salt, flour, and baking powder. Bake for 1 hour 20 minutes to 1 hour 30 minutes, until set. Let cool slightly and serve warm.

Green Tomato Pie
WITH BACON-CHEDDAR CRUST

Makes one 10-inch pie

At the end of one summer, I was left with a load of green tomatoes and wanted to do something with them beyond the usual slice, bread, and fry treatment for sandwiches. I started playing around with a breakfast pie idea, which incorporated just-laid eggs from the hens kept by our local rural mail carrier, Rose, and some thick rashers of applewood-smoked bacon. The Cheddar-y crust speckled with bacon bits was an afterthought, and I initially worried it might be a bit too much. But when I baked off one pie and asked my staff what they thought of it, I got only thumbs up and muffled *mmm*s in reply, because they couldn't even stop chewing to answer me properly. I took that as the best affirmation of all. Green tomatoes work best since they're not full of juice, but ripe red tomatoes can be used if the liquid is drained out—simply slice them and poke your finger through the juicy areas, then let them drain on a paper towel.

CRUST:

½ recipe Savory Pie and Quiche Crust dough (page 102), or 1 store-bought crust

½ cup grated Cheddar cheese

4 bacon slices, cooked and finely chopped

FILLING:

1 tablespoon cornmeal

7 medium green tomatoes, sliced into ⅓-inch-thick rounds

7 bacon slices, cooked and cut into 1-inch pieces

¾ cup mayonnaise

2 large eggs

1½ cups grated Cheddar cheese

1 cup grated Parmesan cheese, plus more for garnish

1 tablespoon unbleached all-purpose flour

⅛ teaspoon cayenne pepper

½ teaspoon smoked paprika

3 scallions, chopped, plus more for garnish

1. **Make the crust:** Sprinkle the Cheddar and bacon bits over the disc of dough. Gently knead them into the dough until evenly incorporated, but don't overwork the dough. Wrap the dough in plastic wrap or put it in a freezer bag and chill for 30 minutes before using.

2. Roll out the pie dough into a 13-inch round, fit it into a 10-inch pie pan, trim, and crimp the edges.

3. Preheat the oven to 350°F. Place a raised wire rack inside a rimmed baking sheet.

4. **Fill the pie:** Sprinkle the cornmeal evenly over the bottom of the pie shell. Layer 3 sliced tomatoes over the bottom. Scatter half the bacon over the tomatoes. Repeat with another layer of 3 sliced tomatoes and the remaining bacon.

5. In a medium bowl, mix together the mayonnaise, eggs, Cheddar, Parmesan, flour, cayenne, paprika, and scallions. Spread the mixture evenly over the filling.

6. Arrange the remaining tomato slices in an attractive pattern on top of the mayonnaise mixture.

7. Place the pie on the prepared baking sheet. Bake for 45 to 60 minutes, turning the baking sheet after 30 minutes, until the exposed filling is golden brown. Let cool for 15 minutes on a raised wire rack before slicing and serving. Garnish with additional chopped scallions and Parmesan cheese, if desired.

MEET OUR PRODUCERS
Jumpin Run
PAGE 216

Savory Pie and Quiche Crust

Makes dough for two 10-inch crusts

This crust is almost identical to our Classic Piecrust (page 60), which is featured in many of our sweet pies. However, this version swaps the sugar and citrus zests for dried sage (you can substitute fresh rosemary), which complements the fillings in our quiches and savory pies.

3½ cups unbleached all-purpose flour, sifted

1 teaspoon kosher salt

¾ cup (1½ sticks) unsalted butter, chilled and cubed

¼ cup vegetable shortening, chilled

1 large egg yolk

½ teaspoon dried sage or chopped fresh rosemary

½ cup cold water, plus more as needed

1. In the large bowl, whisk together the flour and salt. Add the chilled cubed butter and shortening; cut the butter and shortening into the flour mixture using your fingers, two knives, or a pastry blender until broken down into pea-sized pieces. Add the egg yolk and the sage and mix until combined. Gradually add the cold water and mix until the dough comes together. If it's crumbly, add a bit more water 1 teaspoon at a time. If it seems sticky, add a bit more flour.

2. Divide the dough in half and form it into two discs. Wrap each disc in plastic wrap or put them in individual freezer bags, and chill for 30 minutes before use, or freeze the dough for up to 1 month, thawing for 2 hours in the refrigerator before using.

Autumn Quiche
WITH BUTTERNUT SQUASH AND HERBED GOAT CHEESE

Makes one 9-inch quiche

When produce farmer Al Henry starts bringing in squash—usually right after Labor Day—we shift over from our asparagus quiche to this fall version loaded with plenty of herbed goat cheese.

½ recipe Savory Pie and Quiche Crust dough (page 102), or 1 store-bought crust

1 tablespoon Dijon mustard

1 (3-pound) butternut squash, peeled, seeded, and cut into ½-inch pieces (about 4 cups)

1 tablespoon plus 2 teaspoons olive oil

Kosher salt and freshly ground black pepper

1 medium yellow onion, cut into ½-inch dice (about 1 cup)

1 (4- to 5-ounce) log goat cheese, at room temperature

2 teaspoons coarsely chopped fresh rosemary

2 teaspoons coarsely chopped fresh thyme

1 cup half-and-half

2 large eggs

1 cup grated Gruyère cheese

1. Roll out the pie dough to a round 11 inches in diameter. Gently pick up the round without stretching it and lay it in a 9-inch fluted metal or ceramic quiche pan, letting the sides of the round droop over the pan edge while tucking the dough with your fingers against the bottom of the pan. Fold the overhang back over the edge toward the inside of the pan, squeezing it together as you turn the pan to give the top of the crust a bit more thickness. If using a fluted metal pan, run your rolling pin over the pan, pressing to trim the dough against the top edge of the pan, and remove the excess dough.

2. Brush the bottom of the crust with the mustard. Chill until ready to use.

3. Preheat the oven to 400°F.

4. In a medium bowl, toss the butternut squash with 2 teaspoons of the olive oil, and season with salt and pepper. Spread the squash over a baking sheet and roast for 15 minutes, until golden brown. Let cool.

5. Reduce the oven temperature to 375°F. Place a raised wire rack inside a rimmed baking sheet.

6. In a medium skillet, heat the remaining 1 tablespoon olive oil over low heat. When the oil is shimmering, add the onion. Season with salt and pepper. Cook slowly for 10 to 15 minutes, until just translucent. Remove the pan from the heat and let cool.

7. In a small bowl, mash the softened goat cheese with the rosemary and thyme to combine.

8. In a separate small bowl, whisk together the half-and-half, eggs, ½ teaspoon salt, and ½ teaspoon pepper.

9. Place the chilled crust on the prepared baking sheet. Spread the cooled onions evenly over the bottom. Spread the roasted squash over the onions. Evenly distribute spoonfuls of the goat cheese mixture on top. Sprinkle evenly with the Gruyère, then pour the egg mixture on top. Be careful to pour slowly and not to splash the filling over the crust, or it will turn brown as the quiche bakes.

10. Bake for 45 to 60 minutes, turning the baking sheet after 30 minutes, until the filling is set and the crust is a deep brown. Let cool before slicing and serving.

Blue-Ribbon Cookies, Bars, and Candies

Birdseed Cookies

Makes 24 cookies

With no actual birdseed in this recipe, these cookies earned the name because we wanted to create a cookie topped with a medley of the more flavorful seeds we had on hand—black and white sesame seeds, poppy seeds, and aniseed—and they looked like they were covered with birdseed. The seed assortment adds a crunchy quality to the cookies, while the anise imparts a pleasant, slightly licorice tone. They're now one of the most popular cookies at the bakery (my friend Paul Tetreault, the director of Ford's Theatre in DC, always has a stack of them in his freezer). I'm sure you won't be able to stop pecking away at them, either.

4 cups unbleached all-purpose flour, sifted

1½ teaspoons baking powder

1 teaspoon kosher salt

½ teaspoon ground or freshly grated nutmeg

1½ cups (3 sticks) unsalted butter, at room temperature

2½ cups sugar

3 large eggs

1 tablespoon pure vanilla extract

¼ cup white sesame seeds

¼ cup black sesame seeds

¼ cup aniseeds

¼ cup poppy seeds

1. Preheat the oven to 350°F.

2. In a small bowl, whisk together the flour, baking powder, salt, and nutmeg.

3. In the bowl of a stand mixer fitted with the paddle attachment, cream the butter and sugar on medium speed for 2 to 3 minutes, until light and fluffy. Add the eggs one at a time, until incorporated. Add the vanilla. Add the flour mixture and beat until well combined. Cover the bowl with plastic wrap, pressing down to adhere to the surface of the dough, and chill the dough for at least 1 hour and up to 3 hours.

4. In a large bowl, mix together the white and black sesame seeds, aniseeds, and poppy seeds. Portion out 2 rounded tablespoons of dough and, using your hands, form them into balls. Roll the dough balls through the seeds to coat. Place the cookies on two ungreased baking sheets and push down with your palm to flatten them into discs about 3 inches in diameter.

5. Bake the cookies for 14 minutes, turning the baking sheets after 7 minutes, until very lightly browned on the edges. Transfer the cookies to a raised wire rack to cool. Store in an airtight jar or plastic bag for up to 3 days, or freeze in a plastic bag for up to 3 months.

Oatmeal Cranberry Cookies

Makes 24 cookies

Dwight grew up in Sanford, North Carolina, so we often make road trips down that way to visit his sister Karen and aunt Molly, who both still live in the area. As soon as we hit the Tar Heel State, we get off of busy I-95 and cruise the slower back roads. It's a gorgeous, primitive countryside with sprawling cotton fields and dotted with abandoned farmhouses and barns.

These cookies are always my fuel when I'm at the wheel (although I'm sometimes able to save a couple for our arrival at either relative's house). Since they're made with oatmeal and packed with cranberries and raisins, I convince myself they're more of a healthy snack than a sweet treat.

2 cups old-fashioned rolled oats

¾ cup unbleached all-purpose flour, sifted

½ cup dark raisins

¼ cup golden raisins

½ cup dried cranberries

¼ teaspoon baking powder

¼ teaspoon baking soda

½ teaspoon kosher salt

6 tablespoons (¾ stick) unsalted butter, at room temperature

¼ cup packed dark brown sugar

½ cup granulated sugar

2 large eggs

½ teaspoon ground cinnamon

1 teaspoon pure vanilla extract

1. Preheat the oven to 350°F. Line two baking sheets with parchment paper.

2. In a large bowl, whisk together the oats, flour, dark raisins, golden raisins, cranberries, baking powder, baking soda, and salt.

3. In the bowl of a stand mixer fitted with the paddle attachment, cream the butter, brown sugar, and granulated sugar on medium speed for 2 to 3 minutes, until light and fluffy. Add the eggs, cinnamon, and vanilla and beat on medium speed until well incorporated. Reduce the speed to low and gradually add the oat mixture. Mix until combined.

4. Portion out 2 rounded tablespoons of dough and, using your hands, form them into balls. Place the dough balls on the prepared baking sheets, spacing them 1 inch apart. Push down with your palm to flatten them into discs about 1½ inches in diameter.

5. Bake for 12 minutes, turning the baking sheets halfway through, until the cookies are light golden brown but still soft. Let cool on the baking sheets for 5 minutes, then transfer to a raised wire rack to cool completely. Store in an airtight jar or plastic bag for up to 3 days, or freeze in a plastic bag for up to 3 months.

Molasses Cookies

Makes about 36 cookies

I often substitute sorghum syrup for other sweeteners in our recipes, but this is not one of those times; only dark molasses will do here. The tar-thick syrup has a pleasant bite that is well complemented by a covey of cold-weather spices: clove, ginger, nutmeg, and cinnamon. When we start baking off batches of these cookies in early October, Main Street fills up with the aroma (I've smelled them in the post office down the block), so customers know they're in the oven before they even walk through the front door. I think of them as a first taste of the holidays, although hooked customers continue to ask for them year-round.

Nonstick cooking spray

4 cups unbleached all-purpose flour, sifted

2 teaspoons ground cinnamon

1 tablespoon ground ginger

¼ cup chopped crystallized ginger

1 teaspoon ground cloves

2 teaspoons baking soda

½ teaspoon baking powder

1½ teaspoons kosher salt

1 cup vegetable shortening, at room temperature

1 cup (2 sticks) unsalted butter, at room temperature

1½ cups granulated sugar

½ cup molasses

2 large eggs

2 cups Demerara or turbinado sugar

1. Preheat the oven to 350°F. Coat three baking sheets with nonstick spray.

2. In a medium bowl, whisk together the flour, cinnamon, ground ginger, crystallized ginger, cloves, baking soda, baking powder, and salt.

3. In the bowl of a stand mixer fitted with the paddle attachment, cream the shortening, butter, granulated sugar, and molasses on medium speed until light and fluffy, about 3 minutes. Scrape down the sides of the bowl with a spatula, then beat in the eggs on medium speed until smooth. Scrape down the sides of the bowl with a spatula and beat in half the flour mixture on medium speed until smooth. Add the remaining flour and beat until smooth. Cover the bowl with plastic wrap and chill dough for at least 2 hours and up to 8 hours.

4. Put the Demerara sugar in a medium bowl. Portion out 2 rounded tablespoons of dough and, using your hands, roll them into balls. Roll the dough balls through the Demerara sugar to coat. Place them on the prepared baking sheets about 3 inches apart and slightly flatten them with your palm.

5. Bake for 10 minutes, turning the baking sheets halfway through, until the tops are slightly puffy and cracked. Let the cookies cool on the pans for 10 minutes, then transfer to a raised wire rack to finish cooling. Store in an airtight jar or plastic bag for up to 3 days, or freeze in a plastic bag for up to 3 months.

Madeleines
FOR JACQUES PÉPIN

Makes 24 madeleines

My well-connected pal Elaine Chon-Baker sent me a text letting me know that my idol, French chef Jacques Pépin, was in Washington, DC, for an interview and book signing at a Smithsonian museum that evening. She had an extra ticket for me if I could get there in time, and asked if I could bring some snacks for the Pépin family to enjoy before they went onstage. We made Buttermilk Chocolate Chewies (page 119) and, at the last moment, I thought to add authentic madeleines, the traditional French butter cookie, for Jacques.

It was a gutsy move baking these for the best French chef around, but I learned to make them from chef Mark Ramsdell of L'Academie de Cuisine. Mark had been trained by White House pastry chef Roland Mesnier, who gave us the original recipe, and it was one of my favorites. I was elated when Jacques pronounced them "terrific!" and his daughter (and TV costar), Claudine Pépin, said they were the best she's ever had.

Use a metal madeleine pan (we prefer the ones without a nonstick coating) with twelve wells, each about 3¼ by 2 inches. The pans are available online at williams-sonoma.com. Note that if you have only a single mold, you have to thoroughly clean and re-prep it before making the second batch of madeleines.

Nonstick cooking spray

½ cup (1 stick) unsalted butter, melted, for brushing, plus ½ cup (1 stick) unsalted butter, at room temperature

1 cup unbleached all-purpose flour, sifted, plus more for dusting

½ cup granulated sugar

2 teaspoons Meyer lemon zest (or 1 teaspoon lemon zest and 1 teaspoon orange zest)

½ teaspoon pure vanilla extract

2 large eggs, at room temperature

Pinch of kosher salt

1 teaspoon baking powder

Confectioners' sugar, for dusting

1. Coat two madeleine pans with nonstick spray, then brush each mold lightly with the melted butter. Chill the pans for 30 minutes, then sprinkle flour into the molds, tapping out any excess. Return the pans to the refrigerator until ready to fill and bake.

2. In the bowl of a stand mixer, whisk together by hand the granulated sugar and lemon zest. Let sit for a few minutes to allow the citrus flavor to infuse the sugar. Add the remaining ½ cup softened butter and, using the paddle attachment, cream on medium speed until light and fluffy, about 3 minutes. Add the vanilla and mix until blended. Add 1 egg and mix until combined.

(recipe continues)

RED TRUCK BAKERY COOKBOOK

3. In a medium bowl, sift together the flour, salt, and baking powder. Add half the flour mixture to the butter-sugar mixture and beat on low until combined, about 1 minute. Add the remaining egg and mix well. Mix in the remaining flour mixture on medium speed, stopping to scrape down the sides of the bowl as needed, until thoroughly combined, about 1 minute.

4. Preheat the oven to 350°F.

5. With a large spoon and a spatula, scoop the batter into a large piping bag (see Tip). Chill in the refrigerator for a few minutes.

6. Remove the prepared madeleine pans from the refrigerator. Pipe the batter into the molds, filling each two-thirds full, starting at the bottom of the shell shape and running a line of batter up to the top end of the shape, then doubling back halfway to create the bump that signifies a proper madeleine.

7. Bake for 8 to 10 minutes, until just golden brown. Quickly remove the cookies from the molds by turning them over and shaking them out onto a raised wire rack. You may need to use the tines of a fork to gently release them. When cooled, lightly sift confectioners' sugar onto the shell side of the madeleines. Store in an airtight jar or plastic bag for up to 3 days, or freeze in a plastic bag for up to 3 months.

TIP *To make a makeshift piping bag, trim one corner off of a gallon-size zip-top bag with scissors to create an opening between ¼ and ½ inch wide.*

RED TRUCK BAKERY COOKBOOK

Farmhand Cookies
WITH PEANUTS

Makes about 36 cookies

Substantial and satiating, these chunky guys are packed with large Virginia peanuts, Rice Krispies cereal, and milk chocolate chips. They were named when a customer came in for a snack for her crew, asking for "something sweet for my farmhands."

Be sure to use only a spatula or wooden spoon to incorporate these additions, because a stand mixer will pulverize them into dust. When you take the cookies out of the oven, you want a little shine at the centers and some give around the edges. If they cook too long, they will stiffen up and get too crunchy, which will detract from the textures of the mix-ins. Don't fret; they'll keep baking on the cooling racks.

2 cups unbleached all-purpose flour, sifted

2 cups old-fashioned rolled oats (not instant)

¾ teaspoon baking soda

¾ teaspoon baking powder

¾ teaspoon kosher salt

¾ cup (1½ sticks) unsalted butter, at room temperature

½ cup vegetable shortening, at room temperature

1¼ cups packed dark brown sugar

¾ cup granulated sugar

2 large eggs

1 tablespoon pure vanilla extract

2 cups Rice Krispies cereal

2 cups peanuts

2 cups milk chocolate chips

1. Preheat the oven to 350°F.

2. In a large bowl, whisk together the flour, oats, baking soda, baking powder, and salt.

3. In the bowl of a stand mixer fitted with the paddle attachment, cream the butter, shortening, brown sugar, and granulated sugar on medium speed until light and fluffy, about 3 minutes. Add the eggs one at a time, followed by the vanilla, and beat until just combined, about 1 minute. Add the flour mixture and beat until well combined. Using a spatula, stir in the Rice Krispies, peanuts, and chocolate chips by hand until just combined; don't overmix. Cover the bowl with plastic wrap and chill the dough for at least 30 minutes and up to 3 hours.

4. Portion out 2 rounded tablespoons of dough and, using your hands, form them into balls. Place the dough balls on three ungreased baking sheets about 3 inches apart and slightly flatten them with your palm—they will continue to spread while baking.

5. Bake for 12 to 14 minutes, turning the baking sheets halfway through, until golden brown. Transfer the cookies to a raised wire rack to cool. Store in an airtight jar or plastic bag for up to 3 days, or freeze in a plastic bag for up to 3 months.

Persimmon Cookies

Makes 24 cookies

It meant Christmas was coming when our mailman delivered a shoebox full of these puffy cookies, sent by my mom's aunt Helen in early fall each year. The persimmons impart a little tang, which gets boosted with holiday spices and plenty of raisins and walnuts.

   For best results, use soft, overly ripe persimmons, which are usually available in autumn after the first frost at farmer's markets. Look for the Hachiya variety—deep orange orbs with pointed bottoms.

Nonstick cooking spray

2 cups unbleached all-purpose flour, sifted

1 teaspoon baking soda

½ teaspoon ground cloves

½ teaspoon ground cinnamon

½ teaspoon ground or freshly grated nutmeg

½ teaspoon kosher salt

½ cup (1 stick) unsalted butter, at room temperature

1 cup sugar

1 large egg, at room temperature

¾ cup persimmon pulp (from about 2 large persimmons; see Tip)

1 cup raisins

1 cup chopped walnuts

1. Preheat the oven to 350°F. Coat two baking sheets with nonstick spray.

2. In a medium bowl, sift together the flour, baking soda, cloves, cinnamon, nutmeg, and salt.

3. In the bowl of a stand mixer fitted with the paddle attachment, cream the butter and sugar together on medium speed until light and fluffy, about 3 minutes. Beat in the egg and persimmon pulp. Add the flour mixture and beat at low speed until just combined. Stir in the raisins and walnuts by hand. Don't overmix.

4. Drop heaping tablespoons of the batter onto the prepared baking sheets, spacing them 1 to 2 inches apart.

5. Bake for 15 minutes, until lightly browned. Transfer the cookies to a raised wire rack to cool. Store in an airtight jar or plastic bag for up to 3 days, or freeze in a plastic bag for up to 3 months.

TIP *Place ripe persimmons into a zip-top bag and store them in the freezer; it softens the fruit even more. When ready to use, thaw and squeeze out the flesh. One large persimmon yields slightly less than ½ cup pulp.*

Buttermilk Chocolate Chewies

Makes about 36 cookies

These soft, fudgy cookies hide plenty of big chocolate chunks beneath their beautifully cracked tops. The buttermilk adds a delicate kick and a little lift, so they puff up nicely. They're very popular with our weekend crowd: one guy bought a few to eat on the road, but didn't try them until he had driven 15 minutes out of town. We saw him again half an hour later as he circled back to get more; he liked them so much that he bought every one we had in the case.

Don't forget to turn the baking sheet halfway through baking, or else the cookies will turn out hard and fail to live up to their chewy name.

2¼ cups unbleached all-purpose flour, sifted

½ teaspoon baking soda

½ teaspoon kosher salt

½ cup (1 stick) unsalted butter, melted

¾ cup unsweetened cocoa powder

2 cups sugar

¾ cup buttermilk

1½ teaspoons pure vanilla extract

2 cups semisweet chocolate chips

1. Preheat the oven to 350°F.

2. In a small bowl, whisk together the flour, baking soda, and salt.

3. In the bowl of a stand mixer fitted with the paddle attachment, beat together the melted butter, cocoa powder, and sugar on medium speed until well combined, about 2 minutes. Gradually add the buttermilk and vanilla. Add the flour mixture and beat until incorporated. Add the chocolate chips and mix until just combined. Cover the bowl with plastic wrap and chill the dough for at least 30 minutes and up to 3 hours.

4. Portion out 2 rounded tablespoons of dough and, using your hands, form them into balls. Place the dough balls on two ungreased baking sheets about 1½ inches apart and slightly flatten them with your palm—they will continue to spread while baking.

5. Bake for 8 minutes, turning the baking sheets halfway through, until the tops are puffy and slightly cracked. Transfer the cookies to a raised wire rack to cool. Store in an airtight jar or plastic bag for up to 3 days, or freeze in a plastic bag for up to 3 months.

White Chocolate Cherry Bars
WITH ALMONDS

Makes 12 bars

These bars were a happy accident. We were mistakenly shipped an order of dried cherries instead of dried cranberries, so we brainstormed how best to use them. Ryan Glendenning, our lead baker in Warrenton, came up with this recipe, which promptly became one of our classics (as is Ryan herself). We finish these bars off with a drizzle of white icing, which is fun to splash and streak across the top.

Nonstick cooking spray

2 cups unbleached all-purpose flour, sifted

¾ teaspoon baking powder

½ teaspoon baking soda

¾ teaspoon kosher salt

1 cup (2 sticks) unsalted butter, at room temperature

1 cup packed dark brown sugar

½ cup granulated sugar

2 large eggs

¼ teaspoon pure vanilla extract

½ teaspoon pure almond extract

1¼ cups sliced almonds

1 cup white chocolate chips

1 cup dried cherries

2 cups confectioners' sugar

1. Preheat the oven to 325°F. Coat a 9 x 12-inch rimmed baking sheet with nonstick spray.

2. In a medium bowl, whisk together the flour, baking powder, baking soda, and salt.

3. In the bowl of a stand mixer fitted with the paddle attachment, cream the butter, brown sugar, and granulated sugar on medium speed until light and fluffy, about 3 minutes. Add the eggs one at a time, beating on medium speed until just combined after each addition. Scrape down the sides of the bowl, then add the flour mixture and beat on medium speed until combined. Scrape down the sides of the bowl, then add the vanilla and almond extract and beat on medium speed until combined. Stir in the almonds, white chocolate chips, and dried cherries by hand until just combined. Spread the mixture over the prepared baking sheet. Smooth the top with a spatula.

4. Bake for 28 minutes, turning the baking sheet halfway through, until the top is a light golden brown.

5. Meanwhile, in a medium bowl, mix the confectioners' sugar with 2 tablespoons water.

6. Let the bars cool completely, then use a spoon to drizzle the frosting on top in zigzags. Cut into roughly 2¾-inch square bars and serve. Place on a serving plate and cover with plastic wrap; store at room temperature for up to 2 days or refrigerate up to 4 days.

Bourbon Balls

Makes about 60 bourbon balls

Folks asked for this Southern classic the minute we first flipped the open sign, but it took a while to add them to our collection. I raved over others' bourbon ball recipes but didn't want to add another item to our crazy holiday baking schedule. Big mistake. They're now a holiday tradition at the bakery, where we sell gift boxes of them in December, and again at Valentine's Day and Mother's Day.

A good bourbon is essential for success; it's not being cooked out, so each drop is savored. I'm a fan of W.L. Weller Special Reserve, because it's mellow with a smooth honey feel that works well with the dark richness of the pecans and sorghum syrup.

2 cups pecan halves

3 cups coarsely crumbled Birdseed Cookies (page 106, prepared without the seeds) or sugar cookies

¼ cup sugar

½ cup heavy cream

3 tablespoons dark corn syrup

3 tablespoons sorghum syrup

1 teaspoon pure vanilla extract

1¼ cups semisweet chocolate chips

3 tablespoons good bourbon

1. Put 1 cup of the pecans in a food processor and pulse until just coarsely chopped. Transfer to a large bowl and add the cookie crumbs. Pulse the remaining 1 cup pecans until finely chopped, transfer to a small bowl, add the sugar, and stir until combined.

2. In a large saucepan, combine the cream, corn syrup, sorghum syrup, and vanilla and bring to a boil over high heat. Remove the pan from the heat, add the chocolate chips, and mix until the chocolate has melted. Add the cookie crumb mixture and stir, then add the bourbon. Mix thoroughly. Transfer to a large bowl, cover tightly with plastic wrap, and refrigerate for 2 hours.

3. Using a very small (½-ounce) scoop or a spoon, form the chocolate mixture into small balls about 1 inch or so in diameter. Roll them through the sugar-pecan mixture to coat and set aside on a tray.

4. The bourbon balls will keep in an airtight container at room temperature for a few days, refrigerated for up to 1 week, or in the freezer indefinitely.

Strawberry Lemonade Bars

Makes 18 bars

One of my rules is to never pass up a lemonade stand. Any kid that entrepreneurial and enterprising will always get my patronage—and a few extra bucks in their tip jar. I know how hard it is to open your own business, so they deserve any encouragement they can get. These summery bars celebrate those pint-powered pop-ups. Like lemon bars, these are a little on the soft side while nestled on a firm shortbread cookie-type base. The brightness of the strawberry is a sweet companion to the tingling tartness of the lemon.

    Never use frozen strawberries for this recipe. They're not sweet enough, don't have enough flavor, and are too watery, so the filling won't gel.

CRUST:

1¼ cups unbleached all-purpose flour, sifted

½ cup granulated sugar

Zest of 1 lemon

¼ teaspoon kosher salt

10 tablespoons (1¼ sticks) unsalted butter, chilled and cubed

1 large egg yolk

FILLING:

¾ cup (1½ sticks) unsalted butter

1 cup granulated sugar

5 large egg yolks

4 cups stemmed, hulled, and quartered fresh strawberries (about 1 quart)

Zest of 1 lemon

½ cup plus 2 tablespoons lemon juice (from 3 or 4 lemons)

¼ cup cornstarch

Confectioners' sugar, for dusting

1. Preheat the oven to 350°F.

2. Make the crust: In a food processor, combine the flour, granulated sugar, lemon zest, salt, and butter and process until the mixture resembles coarse crumbs. Add the egg yolk and pulse until incorporated.

3. Transfer the dough to a 9 x 13-inch baking pan and press it in evenly. Bake for 17 to 20 minutes, turning the pan after 10 minutes, until very lightly browned. Let the crust cool to room temperature. Leave the oven on.

4. Meanwhile, make the filling: In a medium saucepan, melt the butter over medium-low heat. Remove the pan from the heat. Add the granulated sugar and stir until combined. Let cool slightly, then mix in the egg yolks.

5. In a food processor, combine the strawberries, lemon zest, and lemon juice. Add the cornstarch and pulse to incorporate.

6. Add the strawberry mixture to the butter mixture and cook over medium heat, stirring continuously, for 8 to 10 minutes, until the mixture has thickened to a custard-like consistency and coats the back of a spoon. Pour the strawberry mixture over the cooled crust.

7. Bake for 10 minutes, until the filling has set. Let cool in the pan on a raised wire rack for 20 minutes. Transfer to the refrigerator and let set for 2 to 3 hours. Dust with confectioners' sugar and cut into roughly 2¼ x 3-inch bars. Place on a serving plate and cover with plastic wrap; store at room temperature for up to 2 days or refrigerate up to 4 days.

Virginia Peanut Brittle
with SORGHUM

Makes about 1 pound of brittle

My grandmother Noyes's "Welcome to North Carolina" gesture during my summer visits there was to let me help her make peanut brittle on the stovetop. My first job as a youngster was to simply stir, though she ultimately taught me and trusted me with every step of the process.

Whenever we need peanuts for a recipe, we grab a tin of Belmont Peanuts off our own retail shelves. Grown and roasted by Patsy Marks and her family on their farm in Capon, Virginia, just above the North Carolina border, they have a bold buttery flavor and an underlying savory sensibility. The Virginia variety is the largest type of peanut, so they add a satisfying crunch to complement the brittle's crackle.

Nonstick cooking spray

2 tablespoons unsalted butter

1 cup sugar

½ cup sorghum syrup

½ cup corn syrup

1 teaspoon baking soda

2 cups roasted salted peanuts

1. Line a 9 x 12-inch baking sheet with foil and lightly coat the foil with nonstick spray. Coat a metal offset spatula with nonstick spray.

2. In a large saucepan fitted with a candy thermometer (if you have one), melt the butter over low heat. Increase the heat to medium and add the sugar, sorghum syrup, corn syrup, and baking soda. Cook, stirring continuously with a wooden spoon, until deep golden brown, at least 10 minutes. Continue cooking until the mixture reaches 300°F on the candy thermometer, then remove the pan from the heat. (Alternatively, use a spoon to scoop up a bit of the mixture and dip it in a cup of cold water. When it hardens, remove the pan from the heat.)

3. Quickly add the peanuts to the hot mixture and stir with a wooden spoon until combined. Pour the mixture into the prepared pan, quickly spreading it into an even layer with the prepared offset spatula. Let cool for 30 minutes, then break the brittle into large pieces. Store in an airtight container at room temperature for up to 2 weeks.

MEET OUR
PRODUCERS
Belmont
Peanuts
PAGE 216

Mom's Walnut Chews

Makes 18 bars

These are a remarkable treat: when you cut into a sheet of these chews, the beautifully brittle top flakes into sweet shards, but somehow underneath they're soft and nearly juicy, punctuated with plenty of walnuts. We had a walnut tree in our backyard when I was growing up, which may be the reason my mom was inspired to make these. They soon became a tradition at our house and one of Mom's hallmark snacks, a staple for PTA meetings, Scout get-togethers, and school bake sales. My sisters, Cheryl and Diane, would've been heartbroken not to see these in the book. So, here you go.

Nonstick cooking spray

2 cups packed dark brown sugar

2 large eggs, beaten

1 teaspoon pure vanilla extract

1 cup unbleached all-purpose flour, sifted

¼ teaspoon baking soda

2½ cups walnut halves

1. Preheat the oven to 325°F. Coat a 9 x 13-inch baking sheet with nonstick spray.

2. In the bowl of a stand mixer fitted with the paddle attachment, beat together the brown sugar, eggs, and vanilla until well combined.

3. In a medium bowl, whisk together the flour and baking soda. Add the flour mixture to the brown sugar mixture and beat until combined, scraping down the sides of the bowl as needed. Stir in the walnuts.

4. Pour the batter onto the prepared baking sheet and smooth it out with a spatula. Bake for 20 to 25 minutes, until browned at the edges and beginning to pull away from the sides of the pan. Let cool in the pan, then cut into roughly 2¼ x 3-inch bars. Store in an airtight container at room temperature for up to 2 weeks, or in the freezer for 6 months.

Cakes, Cakes, Cakes

Meyer Lemon Cake

Makes one 10-inch Bundt cake

Once the Christmas rush is over, I am *so* ready to move on to spring. The aroma of Meyer lemons, with a hint of orange and without the tartness of regular lemons, takes me right back to my childhood in California, where groves of sunny citrus trees stretched off in all directions and the air really did smell just like this fruit.

You will need about ten Meyer lemons for all the zest and juice required. Meyer lemons are available from November through May in larger grocery stores, or can be purchased online from whiteflowerfarm.com. Regular lemons can be substituted, but you'll miss the nuances of Meyer lemons.

CAKE:

Nonstick cooking spray

3 cups unbleached all-purpose flour, sifted, plus more for dusting

3 tablespoons grated Meyer lemon zest

2½ cups granulated sugar

1 teaspoon baking soda

½ teaspoon baking powder

1 teaspoon kosher salt

½ cup canola oil

½ cup (1 stick) unsalted butter, at room temperature

6 large eggs

½ cup fresh Meyer lemon juice

1 cup sour cream

SYRUP:

¼ cup fresh Meyer lemon juice

½ cup granulated sugar

GLAZE:

1½ cups confectioners' sugar

1 tablespoon Meyer lemon zest

2 tablespoons fresh Meyer lemon juice

1. Preheat the oven to 350°F. Lightly coat a 10-inch Bundt pan with nonstick spray and dust it with flour, tapping out any excess.

2. Make the cake: In a medium bowl, combine the lemon zest and the granulated sugar with a fork. Let sit for a few minutes to allow the lemon to infuse the sugar.

3. In a separate medium bowl, mix together the flour, baking soda, baking powder, and salt.

4. In the bowl of a stand mixer fitted with the paddle attachment, beat the oil, butter, and the lemon-sugar mixture on medium speed until light and fluffy, about 3 minutes. Add the eggs one at a time, beating well after each addition. Add the lemon juice.

5. With the mixer running on low speed, add the flour mixture in three additions, alternating with the sour cream and beginning and ending with the flour; mix until just blended after each addition.

6. Transfer the batter to the prepared pan. Smooth the top with a spatula. Bake for 50 to 60 minutes, turning the pan after 25 minutes, until a toothpick inserted into the center of the cake comes out clean. Let cool in the pan for 10 minutes, then invert onto a raised wire rack set over a baking sheet to cool.

7. Meanwhile, make the syrup: In a small saucepan, heat the lemon juice, sugar, and ¼ cup water over low heat, stirring, until the sugar has dissolved. Brush the syrup over the cooling cake after removing it from the Bundt pan.

8. Make the glaze: In a small bowl, whisk together the confectioners' sugar, lemon zest, lemon juice, and 1 tablespoon water. After the cake has cooled completely, spoon the glaze over the top of the cake, letting it run down the sides.

MEET OUR
PRODUCERS
Belmont
Farm Distillery
PAGE 216

Double-Chocolate Moonshine Cake

Makes one 10-inch Bundt cake

We get our hooch from a friend in the next county: Ol' Chuck Miller, the first moonshiner to go legal in the Commonwealth of Virginia. Known around these parts as Virginia lightning, moonshine is high-proof, high-intensity corn-distilled whiskey that can send you over the edge if you don't watch out. Luckily, moonshine isn't as overpowering when you bake with it, and I wanted to offer up some kind of hooch cake as a Virginia treat. Its vanilla-like flavor pairs well with chocolate, and the orange zest and nutmeg complement both. Moonshine is available in most liquor stores; don't be tempted by any flavored varieties.

Nonstick cooking spray

1¼ cups unbleached all-purpose flour, sifted

¼ teaspoon baking soda

Pinch of kosher salt

¼ teaspoon ground or freshly grated nutmeg

2½ teaspoons instant vanilla pudding mix

1 tablespoon unsweetened cocoa powder

1 cup packed dark brown sugar

6 tablespoons (¾ stick) unsalted butter, at room temperature

2 tablespoons canola oil

2 large eggs

Heaping 1 cup semisweet chocolate chips, melted

2 tablespoons buttermilk

¼ cup moonshine

1 tablespoon dark rum

¼ teaspoon orange zest

1. Preheat the oven to 350°F. Coat a 10-inch Bundt pan with nonstick spray.

2. In a small bowl, whisk together the flour, baking soda, salt, nutmeg, pudding mix, and cocoa powder.

3. In the bowl of a stand mixer fitted with the paddle attachment, cream the brown sugar and butter until light and fluffy, about 3 minutes. Add the canola oil and eggs and beat until smooth.

4. In a medium bowl, whisk half the melted chocolate chips and the buttermilk until well blended. Whisk in the moonshine, rum, orange zest, and ¼ cup plus 2 tablespoons water until smooth.

5. Add the flour mixture to the butter mixture in three additions, alternating with the buttermilk mixture and beginning and ending with the flour; beat on medium speed until just blended and smooth after each addition.

6. Transfer the batter to the prepared pan. Smooth the top with a spatula. Bake for 45 minutes, turning the pan after 20 minutes, until a toothpick inserted into the center of the cake comes out clean. Let cool completely, then turn the cake out of the pan onto a cake platter or plate.

7. Drizzle the remaining ½ cup melted chocolate over the top of the cake (reheat it briefly if it has set too much to drizzle), letting it run down the sides.

Shenandoah Apple Cake
WITH MAPLE GLAZE

Makes one 10-inch Bundt cake

It's taken me a while to realize just how lucky we were to open up shop on the edge of the Shenandoah Valley: it's apple country here! In the autumn, we'll fire up the old red pickup, crank up some Patsy Cline—this was her homeland—and drive over to Stribling Orchard to pick up jugs of fresh-pressed cider and several crates of apples for our pies and cakes. *Saveur* magazine wrote lovingly of autumn in the Blue Ridge Mountains, the Shenandoah Valley, and our apple cake—stating that we were their favorite of all pastry providers in the area. Bake this at home and you'll get an idea why.

For this recipe, Honeycrisp, Gala, or Granny Smith apples work best.

Nonstick cooking spray

3 cups unbleached all-purpose flour, sifted, plus more for dusting

1 teaspoon baking soda

½ teaspoon baking powder

1 teaspoon kosher salt

1 teaspoon ground cinnamon

½ teaspoon ground or freshly grated nutmeg

½ teaspoon ground ginger

½ cup canola oil

½ cup (1 stick) unsalted butter, cubed, at room temperature

3 cups granulated sugar

6 large eggs

½ cup apple cider or apple juice

1 cup sour cream

2 medium apples (about 2 cups), cored and coarsely chopped

1½ cups confectioners' sugar

2 tablespoons pure maple syrup

1. Preheat the oven to 350°F. Lightly coat a 10-inch Bundt pan with nonstick spray and dust it with flour, tapping out any excess.

2. In a medium bowl, mix together the flour, baking soda, baking powder, salt, cinnamon, nutmeg, and ginger.

3. In the bowl of a stand mixer fitted with the paddle attachment, cream the canola oil, butter, and 2½ cups of the granulated sugar on medium speed until light and fluffy, about 3 minutes. Add the eggs one at a time, beating well after each addition. Add the apple cider.

4. Add the flour mixture in three additions, alternating with the sour cream and beginning and ending with the flour; mix on low until just blended after each addition. Fold in the chopped apples.

5. Transfer the batter to the prepared pan. Smooth the top with a spatula. Bake for 50 to 60 minutes, turning the pan after 30 minutes, until a toothpick inserted into the center of the cake comes out clean. Let cool in the pan for 10 minutes, then invert the cake onto a raised wire rack set over a baking sheet to cool completely.

6. Meanwhile, in a small saucepan, heat the remaining ½ cup granulated sugar and ½ cup water over low heat, stirring until the sugar has dissolved completely. Brush the syrup over the cooling cake after removing it from the Bundt pan.

7. In a small bowl, whisk together the confectioners' sugar, maple syrup, and 2 tablespoons water. After the cake has cooled completely, spoon the glaze over the top of the cake, letting it run down the sides.

MEET OUR
PRODUCERS
The Farm
at Sunnyside
PAGE 214

UPSIDE-DOWN PEAR
Gingerbread Cake

Makes one 9-inch cake

I love gingerbread, and although we bake it each December, I wanted to offer an elevated version for holiday entertaining. My friend Gardiner Lapham at the nearby Farm at Sunnyside brings me excess pears each fall, and they inspired this recipe.

We recommend using a well-greased springform pan to ensure the cake comes out as smoothly as possible. Pieces of pear will inevitably stick to the bottom, but you can easily pop them off the pan with a knife. Comice pears are best for this recipe, though Bartletts and even Asian pears also work well. Make sure they're not too ripe, as they won't hold their shape when baked. You're looking for the fruit to be soft enough that you can push your thumb into it without juice squirting everywhere.

Nonstick cooking spray
Unbleached all-purpose flour, for dusting

TOPPING:

4 tablespoons (½ stick) unsalted butter, melted
3 tablespoons packed dark brown sugar
3 tablespoons chopped crystallized ginger
3 ripe medium pears, peeled, halved, and cored

CAKE:

1 tablespoon grated fresh ginger
2 teaspoons orange zest
½ cup granulated sugar
1¼ cups unbleached all-purpose flour, sifted
½ teaspoon baking powder
½ teaspoon baking soda
½ teaspoon kosher salt
1 tablespoon ground cinnamon
½ teaspoon ground allspice
¼ teaspoon ground or freshly grated nutmeg

2 teaspoons ground ginger
¼ teaspoon ground cloves
2 large eggs
¾ cup buttermilk
½ cup molasses
2 tablespoons canola oil

1. Preheat the oven to 375°F. Coat a 9-inch round cake pan with nonstick spray and dust it with flour, tapping out any excess. To prevent the fruit in the batter from sticking to the pan, line the pan with parchment paper cut to fit and spray the parchment with nonstick spray.

2. Make the topping: Pour the melted butter into the prepared cake pan, tilting it to evenly cover the bottom. Sprinkle the brown sugar and crystallized ginger evenly over the bottom. Holding the pear halves in your palm, slice them lengthwise into ¼-inch-thick slices. Place each half carefully in the pan, rounded-side down, fanning the slices by pressing down. Repeat with each pear half to make a spoke pattern around the pan.

3. Bake for 15 minutes, until the pears look softened and lightly browned.

4. Meanwhile, make the cake: In a small bowl, combine the fresh ginger, orange zest, and granulated sugar and stir with a fork. Let sit for a few minutes to allow the orange and ginger flavors to infuse the sugar.

(recipe continues)

5. In a large bowl, whisk together the flour, baking powder, baking soda, salt, cinnamon, allspice, nutmeg, ginger, and cloves. Add the sugar mixture to the flour mixture.

6. In a separate large bowl, whisk together the eggs, buttermilk, molasses, and canola oil. Add the egg mixture to the flour mixture and stir with a wooden spoon or spatula to combine.

7. When the pears are baked, pour the batter carefully and slowly into the pan over the pears to ensure they maintain their pattern. Bake for 25 to 33 minutes, turning the pan after 15 minutes, until golden brown on top and a toothpick inserted into the center of the cake comes out clean. Let cool in the pan for 15 minutes. Carefully invert the cake onto a large plate or platter and remove the parchment. Let cool completely before slicing and serving.

Orange Olive Oil Cake
WITH ROSEMARY

Makes one 9-inch cake

I love citrus. I love olive oil. I love rosemary. Why can't they all play together in one dessert? I can't say this recipe is at all Southern, unless we're talking about southern Italy. You don't really taste the olive oil, which is there to embellish the cake with a silken quality that lingers on your tongue long after you've polished off a slice. A mellow, full-bodied extra-virgin varietal works best. Don't use anything too punchy or peppery; that will interfere with the bold orange flavor that should be the main focus. This is a sophisticated yet simple cake, just lightly finished with a dusting of confectioners' sugar across the top.

¾ cup olive oil, plus more for greasing

1¾ cups unbleached all-purpose flour, sifted, plus more for dusting

1 tablespoon orange zest

1 tablespoon Meyer lemon zest (or regular lemon zest)

Heaping 1 tablespoon finely chopped fresh rosemary, plus a sprig of fresh rosemary for garnish

1½ cups granulated sugar

1 teaspoon baking powder

½ teaspoon baking soda

¼ teaspoon kosher salt

2 large eggs

¾ cup fresh orange juice

¼ cup fresh Meyer lemon juice

2 tablespoons confectioners' sugar

Thinly sliced orange round, for garnish

1. Preheat the oven to 350°F. Lightly grease a 9-inch round cake pan with olive oil and dust it with flour, tapping out any excess.

2. In a small bowl, combine the orange zest, lemon zest, chopped rosemary, and granulated sugar and stir with a fork. Let sit for a few minutes to let the flavors of the zests and rosemary infuse the sugar.

3. In the bowl of a stand mixer fitted with the whisk attachment, combine the flour, baking powder, baking soda, and salt. Add the sugar mixture and whisk it all together. Add the eggs, orange juice, lemon juice, and olive oil. Mix for 2 minutes on medium speed, until well combined.

4. Transfer the batter to the prepared pan. Smooth the top with a spatula. Bake for 35 to 40 minutes, turning the pan after 20 minutes, until the cake is golden brown and bounces back when touched. Invert the cake onto a cake plate and let cool.

5. Turn the cooled cake over and lightly dust the top with confectioners' sugar. Decorate with a sprig of fresh rosemary and an orange round.

Bourbon Sarsaparilla Cake
WITH CHERRIES AND ALMONDS

Makes one 10-inch Bundt cake

On the urban-bourbon trail in Louisville, Kentucky, Dwight and I grabbed two stools at Proof on Main, the celebrated farm-to-table restaurant in the 21c Museum Hotel. I told the bartender I needed to invent a holiday punch for a local magazine, and challenged him to come up with a cocktail using bourbon, a little almond, and cherry liqueur. He went one better and muddled in some fresh sassafras root. After one taste, I knew we had the punch we were looking for, and thought this could also be the start of a lively cake for the bakery.

We subbed sarsaparilla for the sassafras, but feel free to use root beer—just make sure either is made with pure cane sugar and not high-fructose corn syrup. And it's worth your time to track down Luxardo cherries or Woodford Reserve–soaked cherries rather than using the unnaturally red maraschino cherries.

CAKE:

Nonstick cooking spray

2 tablespoons unsalted butter, at room temperature

¼ cup canola oil

1¼ cups packed dark brown sugar

¼ cup sour cream

¼ cup buttermilk

2 large eggs

1 teaspoon pure vanilla extract

½ cup bourbon

½ cup sarsaparilla or root beer

¼ teaspoon pure almond extract

2½ cups unbleached all-purpose flour, sifted

2 teaspoons instant vanilla pudding mix

¼ teaspoon kosher salt

1 teaspoon baking soda

1 teaspoon baking powder

½ cup Luxardo or Woodford Reserve–soaked cherries, halved

BUTTERCREAM FROSTING:

3 cups confectioners' sugar

¾ cup (1½ sticks) unsalted butter, at room temperature

1½ teaspoons pure vanilla extract or bourbon

1 tablespoon plus 1 teaspoon whole milk

Sliced almonds for garnish

1. Preheat the oven to 350°F. Coat a 10-inch Bundt pan or 9-inch round cake pan with nonstick spray.

2. Make the cake: In the bowl of a stand mixer fitted with the paddle attachment, beat together the butter, canola oil, and brown sugar until light and fluffy, about 3 minutes.

3. In a medium bowl, whisk together the sour cream and buttermilk. Add the eggs and beat until smooth. Add the vanilla and mix until combined. Add the bourbon, sarsaparilla, and almond extract.

4. In a separate medium bowl, whisk together the flour, pudding mix, salt, baking soda, and baking powder.

5. Add the flour mixture to the butter mixture in three additions, alternating with the buttermilk mixture and beginning and ending with the flour; beat on medium speed until just blended and smooth after each addition. Stir in the cherries by hand, but don't overmix.

6. Transfer the batter to the prepared pan. Smooth the top with a spatula. Bake for 45 minutes, turning the pan after 20 minutes, until a toothpick inserted into the center of the cake comes out clean and the middle of the cake bounces back when touched. Let cool completely, then turn the cake out of the pan onto a cake stand or platter.

7. Meanwhile, make the frosting: In the bowl of a stand mixer fitted with the paddle attachment, beat together the confectioners' sugar, butter, vanilla, and milk until smooth.

8. Frost the top of the cake, letting it drip down the sides. Garnish with the sliced almonds.

Mrs. Beavers's Caramel Cake
with APRICOTS

Makes one 9-inch three-layer cake

Longtime residents of The Plains here in Fauquier County talk in reverent tones about local legend Mrs. Beavers's caramel cake. Since she passed away a few years ago, many feared her legendary dessert had departed with her. Luckily, a friend of hers came across a partial recipe and sent it to me in hopes of resurrecting it. Some of the directions weren't entirely clear and relatives questioned some of the procedures listed, but we ultimately devised this version that recalls the spirit of her sweet treat. We couldn't help ourselves: we added apricots for a welcome hit of tartness to offset the cake's ardent sweetness. I hope—and think—Mrs. Beavers would have approved.

CAKE:

Nonstick cooking spray

2½ cups unbleached all-purpose flour, sifted, plus more for dusting

2 cups granulated sugar

½ cup (1 stick) unsalted butter, at room temperature

4 large eggs, separated

1 teaspoon pure vanilla extract

2 teaspoons baking powder

¼ teaspoon kosher salt

1 cup whole milk

12 fresh ripe or canned apricots, coarsely chopped

CARAMEL:

3½ cups packed light brown sugar

1 cup heavy cream

1 cup whole milk

4 tablespoons (½ stick) unsalted butter

1 teaspoon pure vanilla extract

CARAMEL BUTTERCREAM FROSTING:

1 cup (2 sticks) unsalted butter, at room temperature

½ cup plus 1 tablespoon vegetable shortening, at room temperature

½ teaspoon kosher salt

4½ cups confectioners' sugar

1 teaspoon pure vanilla extract

1. Preheat the oven to 375°F. Lightly coat three 9-inch round cake pans with nonstick spray and dust them with flour, tapping out any excess. Line the bottoms with parchment paper cut to fit and spray the parchment with nonstick spray.

2. Make the cake: In the bowl of a stand mixer fitted with the paddle attachment, cream the granulated sugar and butter on medium speed until light and fluffy, about 3 minutes. Add the egg yolks one at a time and beat well; add the vanilla and beat until just combined.

3. In a medium bowl, sift together the flour, baking powder, and salt. Add the flour mixture to the sugar-egg mixture in three additions, alternating with the milk and beginning and ending with the flour; mix until well combined after each addition.

4. In a separate medium bowl using a handheld mixer, beat the egg whites until they hold soft peaks. With a spatula, carefully fold the egg whites into the cake batter.

(recipe continues)

5. Divide the chopped apricots evenly over the bottoms of the prepared pans. Divide the batter evenly among the pans. Bake for 30 minutes, turning the pans after 15 minutes, until the cakes start pulling away from the sides of the pans and a toothpick inserted into the center of the cakes comes out clean. Let cool slightly, then invert the cakes onto a raised wire rack to cool.

6. Make the caramel: In a large saucepan fitted with a candy thermometer (if you have one), combine the brown sugar, cream, milk, butter, and vanilla and stir with a wooden spoon until thoroughly combined. Place the pan over medium-high heat and bring the mixture to a rolling boil; cook, without stirring, for 10 minutes (don't let it burn!). Brush down the sides with a damp pastry brush to prevent sugar crystals from forming. Watch carefully until the mixture reaches 234°F on the thermometer, then remove it from the heat. (Alternatively, spoon up a small bit of the hot caramel and drop it into a glass of cold water—

when it stays in a ball, remove the pan from the heat.) Let cool for 10 minutes.

7. Make the frosting: In the bowl of a stand mixer fitted with the whisk attachment, whip the butter, shortening, ¼ cup of the cooled caramel, and the salt until fully combined. Add the confectioners' sugar and whip until smooth. Add the vanilla and whip until fully combined.

8. Set one cake layer top-side down on a cake plate. Frost just the top of the layer, then add the second cake layer, again top-side down, and frost just the top. Place the third cake layer top-side down on the second. Thickly cover the sides and top of the cake with icing, smoothing it as much as possible with an offset spatula. Refrigerate the cake for 20 minutes.

9. Slightly warm the remaining caramel if it has set while the cake was in the refrigerator and gently pour it over the top of the cake to cover, letting a few drops run down the sides.

Peach Milkshake Cake

Makes one 9-inch two-layer cake

Peach Milkshake Cake—doesn't it sound just like a dessert you would want on your picnic table at a backyard barbecue? The cake is packed with peaches and a touch of vanilla, while the frothy frosting enhanced with malt powder stands in for the whipped cream. Taking a bite recalls all the flavors of a handspun shake without all the slurping.

CAKE:

Nonstick cooking spray

3½ cups unbleached all-purpose flour, sifted, plus more for dusting

1 teaspoon kosher salt

2 teaspoons baking powder

2 teaspoons baking soda

¾ cup (1½ sticks) unsalted butter, at room temperature

2¼ cups granulated sugar

4 large eggs

½ cup plus 3 tablespoons half-and-half

1 teaspoon pure vanilla extract

½ teaspoon pure almond extract

2 cups sliced peeled fresh or thawed frozen peaches (about 3 medium peaches)

FROSTING:

¾ cup confectioners' sugar

3 tablespoons malt powder

1 tablespoon instant vanilla pudding mix

2 cups heavy cream

1. Preheat the oven to 350°F. Coat two 9-inch round cake pans with nonstick spray and dust them with flour, tapping out any excess. To prevent the fruit in the batter from sticking to the pans, line the pans with parchment paper cut to fit and spray the parchment with nonstick spray.

2. Make the cake: In a medium bowl, whisk together the flour, salt, baking powder, and baking soda.

3. In the bowl of a stand mixer fitted with the paddle attachment, cream the butter and granulated sugar on medium speed until light and fluffy, about 3 minutes. Add the eggs one at a time and combine thoroughly. Add the half-and-half, vanilla, and almond extract, and mix well. Add half the flour mixture and beat until combined, then scrape down the sides and bottom of the bowl with a spatula. Add the remaining flour mixture and beat to combine, scraping down the bowl as needed. Add the peaches and mix on medium speed just until the fruit is coarsely chopped.

4. Divide the batter evenly between the prepared pans. Smooth the tops with a spoon. Bake for 40 to 45 minutes, turning the pans after 25 minutes, until a toothpick inserted into the center of the cakes comes out clean. Let cool for 10 minutes, then invert onto a raised wire rack, remove the parchment, and let cool completely.

5. Meanwhile, make the frosting: In a small bowl, whisk together the confectioners' sugar, malt, and pudding mix.

6. In a medium bowl, whip the cream with a handheld mixer until it holds soft peaks. Add the confectioners' sugar mixture in three additions, beating to incorporate after each, until the cream holds stiff peaks.

7. Frost the top of one cake layer, top it with the other layer, then frost the outside of the cake completely.

Guinness Stout and Chocolate Irish Cake
WITH BAILEYS CREAM FROSTING

Makes one 10-inch Bundt cake

After the winter holidays and Valentine's Day, things slow down a bit at the bakery. I wanted to make something for St. Patrick's Day that wasn't green or hokey. This cake, full of dark Guinness stout and Callebaut chocolate, tastes like a big, fat, boozy Oreo cookie. We originally topped it with a fluffy Baileys Irish Cream frosting to look like the head on a pint with the froth running down the sides, but now use Baileys coffee creamer for the same taste and better results. It's a favorite with our customers, including our favorite Irishman, Virginia senator Tim Kaine, who enjoyed it so much he posted thanks with a picture of him and the cake moments before he reduced it to crumbs. Now we send him one every year.

CAKE:

Nonstick cooking spray

1 cup unbleached all-purpose flour, sifted, plus more for dusting

¼ cup canola oil

½ cup Guinness stout

1 tablespoon plus 1½ teaspoons unsalted butter, melted

½ cup unsweetened cocoa powder

1 cup granulated sugar

½ cup sour cream

1 large egg

1½ teaspoons pure vanilla extract

2 teaspoons instant vanilla pudding mix

1 teaspoon baking soda

½ teaspoon baking powder

FROSTING:

1¾ cups confectioners' sugar

¼ cup Baileys Irish Cream coffee creamer

1. Preheat the oven to 350°F. Coat a 10-inch Bundt pan with nonstick spray and dust it with flour, tapping out any excess.

2. Make the cake: In a large bowl, whisk together the canola oil, Guinness, and melted butter until well blended. Whisk in the cocoa powder and granulated sugar.

3. In the bowl of a stand mixer fitted with the paddle attachment, beat together the sour cream, egg, and vanilla at medium speed until just combined. Add the Guinness mixture and mix until combined. Add the flour, pudding mix, baking soda, and baking powder. Beat until smooth.

4. Transfer the batter to the prepared pan. Smooth the top with a spatula. Bake for 35 to 40 minutes, turning the pan after 20 minutes, until a toothpick inserted into the center of the cake comes out clean and the middle of the cake bounces back when touched. Let cool completely, then turn the cake out of the pan onto a cake stand or platter.

5. Meanwhile, make the frosting: In a medium bowl, whisk together the confectioners' sugar and Baileys coffee creamer, adding a bit more confectioners' sugar as needed, until the frosting is pourable. Pour the frosting over the top of the cake and let it run down the sides, but don't cover the cake completely.

Southern Sweet Tea Cake

Makes one 9-inch cake

Road trips in the South mean seeking out the best barbecue. We haven't yet made that dish at the bakery, but we've embraced its partner: sweet tea, a staple at every diner and café in our neck of the woods. I've been trying to pour that thirst-quenching flavor into a cake, but could never get it just right. Things worked out during a drinking session at Vivian Howard's Chef & the Farmer restaurant in Kinston, North Carolina. We told the bartender, "We're bourbon boys," and let him have at it. He made us a cocktail full of sweet tea, lemon, and bourbon; the way the flavors played off each other ended up being the perfect combination for this summery cake.

Don't buy a fancy tea to make this cake; instead, do as Southern eateries do when making their sweet tea: grab the Lipton.

CAKE:

4 tablespoons (½ stick) unsalted butter, at room temperature, plus more for greasing

1½ cups unbleached all-purpose flour, sifted, plus more for dusting

½ cup sugar

Zest of ½ lemon

1 cup buttermilk

3 tablespoons loose black tea (from about 9 bags)

½ teaspoon baking powder

¼ teaspoon baking soda

¾ teaspoon kosher salt

¼ cup honey

1 large egg

2 large egg yolks

1 tablespoon fresh lemon juice

1 tablespoon bourbon

GLAZE:

½ cup sugar

1 teaspoon loose black tea (from about 1 bag)

Thinly sliced lemon round

RED TRUCK BAKERY COOKBOOK

1. Preheat the oven to 350°F. Grease a 9-inch round cake pan with butter and dust it with flour, tapping out any excess.

2. Make the cake: In a small bowl, combine the sugar and lemon zest and stir with a fork. Let sit for a few minutes to let the lemon flavor infuse the sugar.

3. In a small saucepan, warm the buttermilk and tea leaves over low heat for 1 to 2 minutes—do not let it simmer or boil or the mixture will curdle. Remove the pan from the heat and let steep for 10 minutes. Set a fine-mesh strainer over a small bowl and strain the buttermilk, pressing on the tea leaves with a spoon to release as much liquid as possible. Scrape the underside of the strainer and add to the bowl (it's okay if some small bits of tea leaf escape into the bowl). Discard the tea leaves.

4. In a small bowl, whisk together the flour, baking powder, baking soda, and salt.

5. In the bowl of a stand mixer fitted with the paddle attachment, cream the butter and sugar-zest mixture on medium speed until light and fluffy, about 3 minutes. Add the honey, egg, egg yolks, lemon juice, and bourbon and beat on medium speed until just combined.

6. Add the flour mixture to the butter mixture in three additions, alternating with the infused buttermilk and beginning and ending with the flour; beat until combined after each addition.

7. Transfer the batter to the prepared pan. Smooth the top with a spatula. Bake for 30 minutes, turning the pan after 15 minutes, until the cake pulls away from the sides of the pan and a knife inserted into the center of the cake comes out clean. Let cool in the pan for 10 minutes. Run a knife around the edge of the pan and invert the cake onto a raised wire rack to cool completely.

8. Meanwhile, make the glaze: In a small pan, combine ½ cup water, the sugar, and the tea leaves and bring to a low boil over medium heat, stirring, until the sugar has dissolved. Pour the syrup through a fine-mesh strainer set over a bowl to catch the loose tea leaves.

9. Brush the tea glaze onto the lemon round.

10. Brush the top and sides of the cake with the tea glaze while it's still warm. Garnish the center of the cake with the glazed lemon slice.

Almond Cake

Makes one 9-inch cake

Originally created as an Easter treat, our Almond Cake quickly became a favorite with customers, who insisted we offer it year-round. It is the perfect showcase for the ambrosial amaretto made by our local Mt. Defiance Distillery.

This cake is so moist that I thought it might be a good candidate to recreate in a gluten-free version. We substituted Cup4Cup gluten-free flour, available at many grocery stores and online, for all-purpose, and the cake was a big hit when introduced at the Garden & Gun Jubilee in Charleston, South Carolina. If you don't want to make the cake gluten-free, you can sub in unbleached all-purpose flour.

Nonstick cooking spray

1 cup almond paste, pulled apart into pieces

3 tablespoons amaretto

¼ teaspoon pure almond extract

½ teaspoon pure orange extract

½ teaspoon pure vanilla extract

1 cup sugar

6 tablespoons (¾ stick) unsalted butter, at room temperature

4 large eggs

½ cup Cup4Cup gluten-free flour, sifted

¾ teaspoon baking powder

½ cup apricot jam

2 tablespoons confectioners' sugar (optional)

1. Preheat the oven to 325°F. Coat a 9-inch round cake pan with nonstick spray.

2. In the bowl of a stand mixer fitted with the paddle attachment, beat the almond paste, amaretto, almond extract, orange extract, and vanilla on medium-high speed until well combined, about 3 minutes. Add the sugar and beat until well incorporated. Add the butter and beat until fluffy. Add the eggs and beat until well incorporated. Add the flour and baking powder and mix until well incorporated.

3. Transfer the batter to the prepared pan. Smooth the top with a spatula. Bake for 40 minutes, turning the pan after 20 minutes, until a toothpick inserted into the center of the cake comes out clean. Turn the cake out onto a raised wire rack to cool.

4. Warm the apricot jam in a small saucepan over low heat or in the microwave until it thins out, and then brush a layer of the jam over the cake while it's still warm.

5. If desired, dust the edges of the cake with the confectioners' sugar using a small sifter or strainer (we first invert a scalloped tart pan and dust around it, then carefully remove it).

MEET OUR PRODUCERS
Mt. Defiance Cidery & Distillery
PAGE 214

Jubilee Cake
WITH COCONUT

Makes one 9-inch two-layer cake

I yearned for a celebratory coconut cake in our repertoire that we could whip up for birthdays, dinner parties, and anniversaries. However, I didn't want to simply do a riff on a hummingbird cake, the banana-boosted pineapple cake popular below the Mason-Dixon Line. I came across a heralded Edna Lewis recipe for coconut cake, which I crossed with a *tres leches* cake by adding a mixture of condensed and coconut milks. The end result couldn't be coconuttier and looks beautiful when topped with frothy peaks of cream cheese icing. Top it off with those long, thin, colorful birthday candles, and you have a party on a plate.

CAKE:

Nonstick cooking spray

2½ cups unbleached all-purpose flour, sifted, plus more for dusting

1 cup granulated sugar

½ cup (1 stick) unsalted butter, at room temperature

4 large eggs, separated

1 teaspoon pure vanilla extract

½ teaspoon pure coconut extract

2 teaspoons baking powder

¼ teaspoon kosher salt

1 cup whole milk

½ cup sweetened condensed milk

1½ cups sweetened shredded or flaked coconut

GLAZE:

½ cup sweetened condensed milk

½ cup coconut milk

1 teaspoon pure coconut extract

FROSTING:

2 (8-ounce) packages cream cheese, at room temperature

1 cup (2 sticks) unsalted butter, at room temperature

¾ teaspoon pure vanilla extract

¼ teaspoon pure coconut extract

5 cups confectioners' sugar

2½ cups sweetened shredded coconut, for garnish

1. Preheat the oven to 375°F. Lightly coat two 9-inch round cake pans with nonstick spray and dust them with flour, tapping out any excess. Line the bottoms with circles of parchment paper cut to fit and spray the parchment with nonstick spray.

2. Make the cake: In the bowl of a stand mixer fitted with the paddle attachment, cream the granulated sugar and butter until light and fluffy, about 3 minutes. Add the egg yolks one at a time and beat well to combine. Add the vanilla and coconut extract and beat well.

3. In a medium bowl, sift together the flour, baking powder, and salt.

4. In a small bowl, whisk together the whole milk and condensed milk.

5. Add the flour mixture to the butter mixture in three additions, alternating with the milk mixture and beginning and ending with the flour; mix until combined after each addition.

6. In a separate medium bowl using a handheld mixer, beat the egg whites until they hold soft peaks and, using a spatula, carefully fold them into the cake batter.

7. Divide the batter evenly between the prepared pans. Bake for 30 minutes, turning the pans after 15 minutes, until the cakes start pulling away from the sides of the pans and a toothpick inserted into the center of the cakes comes out clean. Let cool slightly, then invert the cakes onto a raised wire rack set over a baking sheet. Remove the parchment.

8. **Meanwhile, make the glaze:** In a small bowl, whisk together the condensed milk, coconut milk, and coconut extract. With a fork or skewer, carefully poke holes halfway through the cakes' bottoms while they are still warm. Brush the glaze across the tops and sides of both cakes until they are moistened.

Repeat until you have used all the glaze. Let the cakes cool to allow the glaze to soak in completely.

9. **Make the frosting:** In the bowl of a stand mixer fitted with the paddle attachment, beat together the cream cheese, butter, vanilla, and coconut extract on low speed until well combined. Add the confectioners' sugar and mix until just smooth.

10. To frost the cake, place one cake layer top-side down on a serving plate and spread frosting over just the top. Place the second layer on top, again with the top side down, and frost just the top. Sprinkle with the coconut.

ALMA HACKNEY'S
Rum Cake

Makes one 10-inch Bundt cake

Alma Hackney, the choir director at Dwight's family church—the First Presbyterian Church in Sanford, North Carolina—was beloved for her rum cake, which was always waiting for Dwight when he came home at Christmas. Featuring a yellow cake that would make Betty Crocker proud, it's covered with a crackly rum glaze. She passed the recipe along to Dwight's mother, Dot, who shared it with me, and I promised not to change a thing. The key to this cake is the quality of the rum. The darker the rum, the deeper the flavor, so well-aged golden or dark rum works best.

CAKE:

Nonstick cooking spray

3 cups unbleached all-purpose flour, sifted, plus more for dusting

2 teaspoons instant vanilla pudding mix

1 teaspoon baking soda

½ teaspoon baking powder

1 teaspoon kosher salt

½ cup canola oil

½ cup (1 stick) unsalted butter, at room temperature

2½ cups sugar

6 large eggs

½ cup dark rum

1 cup sour cream

GLAZE:

½ cup (1 stick) unsalted butter

1 cup sugar

¼ cup dark rum

1. Preheat the oven to 350°F. Coat a 10-inch Bundt pan with nonstick spray and dust it with flour, tapping out any excess.

2. Make the cake: In a large bowl, mix together the flour, pudding mix, baking soda, baking powder, and salt.

3. In the bowl of a stand mixer fitted with the paddle attachment, beat together the canola oil, butter, and sugar until light and fluffy, about 3 minutes. Add the eggs one at a time, beating well after each addition. Add the rum and mix until combined.

4. Add the flour mixture to the butter mixture in three additions, alternating with the sour cream and beginning and ending with the flour; mix on low speed until just blended after each addition.

5. Transfer the batter to the prepared pan. Smooth the top with a spatula. Bake for 50 to 60 minutes, turning the pan after 25 minutes, until a toothpick inserted into the center of the cake comes out clean. Let cool in the pan for 10 minutes, then invert the cake onto a raised wire rack set over a baking sheet to cool completely.

6. Meanwhile, make the glaze: In a small saucepan, combine the butter, sugar, and rum and heat over low heat, stirring, until thoroughly combined.

7. Brush the glaze over the cooling cake after removing it from the Bundt pan. Repeat until you have used all the glaze.

Breads

UNCLE STAN'S
Harvest Wheat

Makes two 8½ x 4½-inch loaves

After a spirited back and forth with my uncle Stan over the better part of a year, we nailed this harvest wheat bread, punctuated with golden raisins, dried cranberries, and walnuts. It's been on the bakery's daily list since we opened.

This loaf works well as sandwich bread—we use it for our Chicken Salad with Apples, Grapes, Walnut, and Curry (page 206)—or simply slathered with butter while it's still warm. To keep the loaf soft and springy, and to prevent it from becoming too dense, we use a combination of whole wheat and high-gluten bread flours.

Bread dough is living and growing, and you want to move it about carefully or it will collapse. Don't bang the side of the oven with the loaf pan and be careful to set it down gingerly on the rack.

Nonstick cooking spray

¾ cup warm water

1¼ cups plus 3 tablespoons whole milk

3 tablespoons active dry yeast (four ¼-ounce packets)

¾ cup honey

6 tablespoons (¾ stick) unsalted butter, at room temperature

1½ cups All-Bran cereal

3½ cups bread flour, sifted

2¼ cups whole wheat flour, sifted

½ cup mixed seeds (a combination of sunflower seeds, flaxseed, sesame seeds, and poppy seeds, or any pre-packed mixed grains), plus more for sprinkling

¼ cup old-fashioned oats, plus more for sprinkling

2 tablespoons plus 2 teaspoons kosher salt

¼ cup plus 2 tablespoons dried cranberries

¼ cup plus 2 tablespoons golden raisins

¼ cup plus 2 tablespoons chopped walnuts

1 large egg, whisked with 1 tablespoon water

1. Coat two 8½ x 4½-inch loaf pans with nonstick spray.

2. In the bowl of a stand mixer fitted with the dough hook attachment, whisk together the water, milk, and yeast. Let stand for 10 minutes, until the mixture starts to foam and bubble.

(recipe continues)

3. Add the honey, butter, bran cereal, bread flour, whole wheat flour, mixed seeds, and oats to the yeast mixture and mix on low speed for 6 minutes. Scrape down the sides with a spatula as needed. Add the salt and mix on medium-high speed for 10 minutes. Add the cranberries, raisins, and walnuts and mix on low speed for 6 minutes. Cover the bowl with plastic wrap, place in a warm, draft-free place, and allow the dough to rise for 1½ to 2 hours, until it has risen out of the pan to create a dome and has developed "shoulders" that spill over the side.

4. Turn the dough out onto a surface coated with nonstick spray. Divide the dough into two balls.

5. Using your hands, roll one ball out into a rectangle the width of your bread pan with the long edge facing you. Fold the top half of the dough over toward you halfway across the dough, smashing it down with your palms to eliminate any air holes and pinching the sides and seam together

tightly with your fingers. Bring the bottom half of the dough up to the top, again pressing firmly and pinching all seams. Turn the dough over, evening out the sides with your palms, and place it seam-side down into one of the loaf pans. Repeat with the second ball of dough.

6. Lightly brush the top of each loaf with egg wash (don't let it drip down the sides or it will cause the bread to stick to the pan), sprinkle with seeds or oats, and cover lightly with plastic wrap. Set the loaves in a warm, draft-free space to rise for 1½ to 2 hours, until doubled in size (it may take longer depending on room temperature and humidity; be patient). Make sure the shoulders of the loaf have formed: you want a high dome with a bit of overhang above the pan, but don't let it get too large. If it gets too tall—overflowing and full of air—it will collapse once it hits the heat of the oven.

7. Preheat the oven to 350°F.

8. Bake the loaves for 15 minutes, turn the pans, and bake for 15 to 25 minutes more, until the bread is a dark golden brown, almost mocha, color. Remove the pans from the oven and let cool slightly on a raised wire rack. Run a knife around the edge of each loaf and flip them out of the pans onto their sides on the rack. After 10 minutes, set the loaves upright and let them cool completely before slicing with a serrated bread knife. Store in a plastic bag at room temperature for up to 3 days, or freeze for up to 4 months.

TIP *To allow the bread to rise, place it in a warm spot in your kitchen, such as near the stove or on top of the refrigerator.*

Pumpkin Bread

Makes two 8½ x 4½-inch loaves

This moist loaf is full of pumpkin, walnuts, raisins, and spices. Keep some softened butter handy, so that when the bread cools just enough to slice, you can spread some on. Treat this bread as a blank canvas: oftentimes we'll top these loaves with dried cranberries and roasted pumpkin seeds just before baking, but you can experiment with other nut, dried fruit, or spice toppings.

Nonstick cooking spray

2¾ cups unbleached all-purpose flour, sifted, plus more for dusting

2 cups sugar

½ cup plus 2 tablespoons canola oil

1 cup pure pumpkin puree

3 tablespoons apple cider

½ teaspoon pure vanilla extract

3 large eggs

¾ teaspoon baking powder

2 teaspoons baking soda

1½ teaspoons kosher salt

¾ teaspoon ground cinnamon

¾ teaspoon ground allspice

¾ teaspoon ground ginger

⅛ teaspoon ground cloves

¾ cup walnuts, coarsely chopped, plus (optional) more for topping

¾ cup golden raisins, plus (optional) more for topping

¾ cup dried cranberries, plus (optional) more for topping

1. Preheat the oven to 350°F. Coat two 8½ x 4½-inch loaf pans with nonstick spray and dust them with flour, tapping out any excess.

2. In the bowl of a stand mixer fitted with the paddle attachment, beat together the sugar and the canola oil on medium speed until light and fluffy, about 3 minutes. Scrape down the sides with a spatula, then add the pumpkin and apple cider and mix until well combined. Scrape the sides again before adding the vanilla. Add the eggs one at a time and mix until combined.

3. In a medium bowl, whisk together the flour, baking powder, baking soda, salt, cinnamon, allspice, ginger, and cloves. Add the flour mixture to the pumpkin mixture and mix well. Add the walnuts, golden raisins, and cranberries and mix by hand to combine.

4. Evenly divide the batter between the prepared loaf pans. Smooth the tops with a spatula and sprinkle the loaves with the topping(s) of your choice, if desired. Bake for 45 to 60 minutes, until deep golden brown and a knife inserted into the center comes out clean. Let cool slightly in the pan, then flip onto a wire rack to cool completely.

Banana Bread
WITH WALNUTS AND CHOCOLATE

Makes two 8½ x 4½-inch loaves

Don't throw out bananas once they've blackened; instead, keep them in your freezer, unpeeled, for this recipe (or hit up the local grocery stores for dark, bruised bananas that are pulled from the shelf; we often find them for a buck per pound). The sugar in overripe bananas is highly concentrated, so they're super sweet and extra flavorful. This bread can be thrown together in a jiffy, so it's the perfect solution for a just-remembered school bake sale or a spur-of-the-moment get-together with friends.

If using frozen bananas, let them thaw slightly until softened, but still chilled. Then squeeze them from their peels directly into the mixer and beat as directed.

Nonstick cooking spray

3¼ cups unbleached all-purpose flour, sifted, plus more for dusting

1¼ cups sugar

3 tablespoons unsalted butter, at room temperature

6 overripe bananas, cut into 1-inch pieces

2 tablespoons buttermilk

¾ cup canola oil

½ teaspoon pure vanilla extract

4 large eggs

½ teaspoon baking powder

1 tablespoon baking soda

½ teaspoon kosher salt

1 cup coarsely chopped walnuts

1 cup semisweet chocolate chips

1. Preheat the oven to 350°F. Coat two 8½ x 4½-inch loaf pans with nonstick spray and dust them with flour, tapping out any excess.

2. In the bowl of a stand mixer fitted with the paddle attachment, cream together the sugar and the butter on medium-high speed until light and fluffy, about 3 minutes. Add the bananas and mix until well combined. Add the buttermilk, canola oil, vanilla, and eggs, mixing well and scraping down the sides of the bowl with a spatula as needed.

3. In a medium bowl, whisk together the flour, baking powder, baking soda, and salt. Add the flour mixture to the banana mixture and mix on low until well blended. Mix in the walnuts and chocolate chips.

4. Divide the batter evenly between the prepared pans. Smooth the tops with a spatula. Bake for 50 to 60 minutes, until deep golden brown and a knife inserted into the center comes out clean. Let cool slightly in the pan, then flip onto a raised wire rack to cool completely.

RED TRUCK BAKERY COOKBOOK

Focaccia
WITH FRESH ROSEMARY

Makes one 9-inch focaccia

If you've never made a loaf of bread before, this recipe is a good place to start. You make this bread on the day you eat it; no advance prep work required. Topped with crunchy crystals of sea salt and fresh rosemary that we grow right outside our Warrenton location, it's perfect for sandwiches. My favorite combo is thick-sliced Black Forest ham, slabs of white Cheddar cheese, a couple leaves of Boston lettuce, and a hearty swipe of honey mustard.

Use a stand mixer fitted with a dough hook to knead the dough, if you like, but we find it more satisfying to knead by hand.

2¼ teaspoons active dry yeast (one ¼-ounce packet)

1 cup warm (not hot) water

1½ cups bread flour, sifted

Olive oil

½ teaspoon kosher salt

1½ cups unbleached all-purpose flour, sifted

Nonstick cooking spray

3 tablespoons chopped fresh rosemary, for sprinkling

Sea salt, for sprinkling

1. In the bowl of a stand mixer fitted with the paddle attachment, dissolve the yeast in the warm water. Add 2 tablespoons of the bread flour, whisk well, and let stand until foamy, about 10 minutes.

2. Add 1 tablespoon olive oil, the salt, and the remaining bread flour. Start mixing on low-medium speed, adding the all-purpose flour ½ cup at a time, until the dough starts to pull away from the sides of the bowl (you may not need to add all of it, though if it's a humid day, you may need to add a bit more).

3. At this point you can continue working the dough in the mixer with the bread hook, adding more flour as necessary, until it feels smooth, about 10 minutes. Alternatively, turn the dough out onto a lightly floured surface and knead by hand, adding more flour if necessary, until the dough feels smooth, about 15 minutes.

4. Coat a large bowl with olive oil, form the dough into a ball, and place it in the bowl. Gently turn the dough over to coat all sides with oil. Cover with plastic wrap or a damp kitchen towel and let rise in a warm, draft-free space for 1½ to 2 hours, until doubled in size.

5. Preheat the oven to 425°F. Coat a 9-inch round cake pan with nonstick spray.

6. Punch down the dough and turn it out onto a lightly floured surface. Pat out the dough into a large, thin circle about 7 inches wide and place it in the prepared pan. Brush the top well with olive oil. Cover again and let rise in a warm, draft-free space for 30 minutes, until doubled in size.

7. Bake for 23 to 28 minutes, until the focaccia is lightly browned and puffed up. Immediately brush with more olive oil and sprinkle with chopped rosemary and sea salt. Slide a fork underneath the focaccia to ease it out of the pan and onto a raised wire rack to cool. Store in a plastic bag for 3 days at room temperature, or in the freezer for up to 1 month.

SORGHUM-GLAZED
Pecan Pull-Aparts

Makes one 10-inch pull-apart bread

When I was a kid, every Saturday morning my dad would drive me and my brothers Mark and Doug to a nearby grocery store to buy freshly baked pull-aparts (similar to sticky buns and monkey bread) as a weekend breakfast treat for the family. When we got back to the house, all seven of us would gather around the table, rip off pieces, and wolf them down as we passed around sections of the newspaper. This Southern-style pull-apart bread pays homage to that gloriously gooey breakfast ritual.

Unless you plan on getting up several hours before everyone else, make these the day before you want to serve them. Right before you eat, pop them back in the oven at 250°F for 20 minutes to warm up.

DOUGH:

6 tablespoons (¾ stick) unsalted butter

¾ cup whole milk

2 tablespoons granulated sugar

2 teaspoons instant yeast (from one ¼-ounce packet)

1 large egg

1 large egg yolk

1 teaspoon kosher salt

2¼ cups unbleached all-purpose flour, sifted, plus more as needed

Nonstick cooking spray

SORGHUM GLAZE AND TOPPINGS:

1 cup (2 sticks) unsalted butter

1 cup granulated sugar

1 tablespoon ground cinnamon

Nonstick cooking spray

1½ cups coarsely chopped pecans

6 tablespoons packed dark brown sugar

½ cup sorghum syrup

1 teaspoon honey

1 teaspoon kosher salt

1 teaspoon pure vanilla extract

1. **Make the dough:** In a medium saucepan, melt the butter over medium heat. Add the milk and granulated sugar and stir with a wooden spoon until the sugar has dissolved and the ingredients are combined. Remove the pan from the heat, let cool, then pour the mixture into a large bowl. Stir in the yeast and let sit for 15 minutes, until foamy.

2. In a large bowl, beat together the egg and egg yolk, then add them to the milk mixture. Add the salt. Add the flour a bit at a time, mixing first with a wooden spoon and then with your hands as the dough becomes heavier, until you have a smooth ball. Add more flour as needed.

3. Coat a large bowl with nonstick spray and place the dough in the bowl. Coat the top of the dough with spray as well. Cover with plastic wrap or a damp kitchen towel and let rise in a warm, draft-free place for 1 hour 30 minutes, until doubled in size.

4. In a small saucepan, melt ½ cup (1 stick) of the butter over medium-low heat and set aside to cool.

5. In a small bowl, mix together the granulated sugar and cinnamon.

(recipe continues)

RED TRUCK BAKERY COOKBOOK

6. Coat a 10-inch Bundt pan with nonstick spray and sprinkle in a third of the pecans. Punch the dough down. Pull off golf ball–sized pieces and roll them into balls with your hands. Dip each ball in the melted butter, then roll it through the cinnamon sugar and put the coated ball over the layer of pecans in the Bundt pan. Repeat until you have one layer of dough (you'll use about half the dough balls). Add another third of the pecans, then repeat with the remaining dough balls and pecans. Cover with plastic wrap or a damp kitchen towel and let rise in a warm, draft-free place (not the oven) for 1 hour, until the dough has expanded to fill three-quarters of the pan.

7. Meanwhile, make the sorghum glaze: In a medium saucepan, melt the remaining ½ cup (1 stick) of the butter over medium heat. Stir in the brown sugar, sorghum syrup, honey, salt, and vanilla until well combined and starting to bubble.

8. Preheat the oven to 350°F.

9. Reheat the sorghum glaze if necessary (but don't let it get too hot) and pour it over the risen dough balls. Place the Bundt pan on a rimmed baking sheet and bake for 40 to 50 minutes, until the top layer of pull-aparts is deep brown. Let cool for 10 minutes, then invert onto a plate and serve immediately.

OLD-WORLD
Almond Stollen

Makes four 4 x 7-inch loaves

Families have returned from summer vacation, kids are headed back to school, and our phones start to ring with questions about how soon we'll be baking our stollen. September's way too early to start our old-world stollen, a buttery loaf of raisins, citrus, and almonds wrapped around an almond log, which we bake only in December. I knew it had a loyal following when a concerned New Yorker called us up wondering if our stollen "was like the one at that place in Lawng Guyland." She called back a week later with an update after receiving a loaf: "It's even bettah!"

FILLING:

1 cup almond paste (8 ounces)

½ cup granulated sugar

1 large egg white

1¾ cups sliced almonds

Unbleached all-purpose flour, for dusting

SPONGE:

¾ cup lukewarm whole milk

5 teaspoons active dry yeast

1½ cups bread flour, sifted

⅛ teaspoon kosher salt

Nonstick cooking spray (optional)

DOUGH:

1 tablespoon plus 1 teaspoon almond paste (about 1 ounce)

½ teaspoon pure vanilla extract

Finely grated zest of 1 orange

2 tablespoons plus 2 teaspoons granulated sugar

1 cup (2 sticks) unsalted butter, cubed, at room temperature

1¾ cups bread flour, sifted

⅛ teaspoon kosher salt

1 cup Candied Citrus Peel (page 201)

1 cup dark raisins

1 cup golden raisins

1¼ cups sliced almonds

ASSEMBLY:

¾ cup granulated sugar

¾ cup confectioners' sugar

½ cup clarified butter, warmed, or ½ cup (1 stick) unsalted butter, melted and strained

1. **Make the filling:** In the bowl of a stand mixer fitted with the paddle attachment, combine the almond paste and granulated sugar and beat on medium speed until well combined. Gradually add the egg white and beat to incorporate. Scrape down the sides of the bowl as needed.

2. Add the sliced almonds and beat on low speed just until evenly distributed, taking care not to crush them completely. Turn the filling out onto a lightly floured surface and divide it into four equal portions, then roll each one into a rounded log about 5 inches long.

3. **Make the sponge:** In the clean bowl of a stand mixer fitted with the paddle attachment, combine the milk, yeast, bread flour, and salt and beat on low speed until well incorporated, then cover with plastic wrap and let sit at room temperature for 30 minutes, until the sponge has doubled in size. (If you have only one stand mixer bowl, transfer the dough to a large bowl coated with nonstick spray and let rise as instructed.)

(recipe continues)

RED TRUCK BAKERY COOKBOOK

4. **Meanwhile, make the dough:** In the clean bowl of a stand mixer fitted with the paddle attachment, combine the almond paste, vanilla, orange zest, and about a third of the granulated sugar and beat on medium-low speed until incorporated, then add the remaining granulated sugar and beat on medium-low speed until blended. Scrape down the sides of the bowl as needed. With the mixer running on medium-low speed, gradually add the butter and beat until just incorporated. Do not overmix.

5. Switch to the dough hook. Add the sponge, bread flour, and salt and beat on low speed for 4 minutes, then increase the speed to high and beat for 2 minutes, until well mixed. Cover the bowl with plastic wrap and let the dough rest at room temperature for 30 minutes.

6. Preheat the oven to 350°F with the racks in the upper and lower thirds of the oven. Line two baking sheets with parchment paper.

7. Uncover the bowl and add the candied citrus peel, dark raisins, golden raisins, and almonds. Mix on the lowest speed for up to 2 minutes to evenly distribute the mix-ins, but not so long that you break up the raisins and almonds.

8. Turn the dough out onto a clean surface. Divide the dough into four equal balls. Use your hands to pat one ball into an oval about 8 x 6 inches. Place a log of almond filling lengthwise in the center of the dough oval and wrap the dough tightly around the log, almost like a soft taco, pinching the sides together along the entire length. Pat the seams smooth, then flip the loaf over and flatten it slightly. You'll have a stollen shaped like a flat football, about 4 x 7 inches and 2 inches high. Repeat with the remaining dough and filling.

9. Arrange two stollen on each of the prepared baking sheets. Let rest in a slightly warm area for about 20 minutes. Bake for 25 to 30 minutes, turning the pans after 15 minutes and transferring the pan on the top rack to the bottom rack, and vice versa, until golden brown. The stollen will not rise much. Let the loaves cool slightly.

10. To assemble, rub off any burnt nuts and raisins. Whisk together the granulated sugar and confectioners' sugars in a medium bowl.

11. Brush the stollen with warm clarified butter, covering every bit of them. Immediately sprinkle some of the mixed sugar over the top, bottom, and sides of each buttered stollen, taking care not to break the warm loaves; there should be enough sugar to coat each loaf completely.

12. Let cool completely, then wrap each loaf in plastic wrap, enclose individually in plastic bags, and gift-box as desired. Stollen will keep at room temperature for up to 4 weeks, or in the freezer for up to 6 months.

Lemon Poppy Seed Tea Bread

Makes one 8½ x 4½-inch loaf

When it comes to our baked goods, we try to stay as seasonal and local as possible. January, however, doesn't offer up much in the way of produce, and by then we're all yearning for a taste of spring. We start making this simple lemon quick bread as soon as we flip the calendar to the new year, and continue offering it through the end of the summer. It's a popular hostess gift for new neighbors or to cheer up a friend, and it's great with hot tea or coffee. To make it even more decadent, after brushing with the glaze, top it with our Meyer Lemon Cake frosting (page 132).

Since the lemon is so important here, definitely use fresh juice, not the bottled stuff.

BREAD:

Nonstick cooking spray

1 cup granulated sugar

1 tablespoon lemon zest

¼ cup fresh lemon juice

1 cup buttermilk

2¼ cups unbleached all-purpose flour, sifted

1 teaspoon baking powder

¼ teaspoon baking soda

½ teaspoon kosher salt

4 tablespoons (½ stick) unsalted butter, at room temperature

2 tablespoons canola oil

2 large eggs

½ cup coarsely chopped crystallized ginger

1 tablespoon poppy seeds

GLAZE:

½ cup granulated sugar

2 teaspoons lemon zest

¼ cup fresh lemon juice

1. Preheat the oven to 350°F. Coat an 8½ x 4½-inch loaf pan with nonstick spray.

2. Make the bread: In a small bowl, combine the granulated sugar and lemon zest. Let sit for a few minutes to let the zest infuse the sugar with citrus flavor.

3. In a separate small bowl, mix together the lemon juice and buttermilk.

4. In a medium bowl, mix together the flour, baking powder, baking soda, and salt.

5. In the bowl of a stand mixer fitted with the paddle attachment, beat together the butter, canola oil, and sugar-zest mixture on medium speed until light and fluffy, about 3 minutes. Add the eggs one at a time, mixing well after each addition.

6. Add the flour mixture to the butter mixture in three additions, alternating with the buttermilk mixture and beginning and ending with the flour; beat well after each addition. Stir in the chopped ginger and poppy seeds by hand.

7. Transfer the batter to the prepared pan. Smooth the top with a spatula. Bake for 50 to 55 minutes, until a toothpick inserted into the center comes out clean. Let cool for 5 minutes in the pan. Run a knife around the inside edge to loosen the bread, then flip it onto a raised wire rack to cool completely.

8. Meanwhile, make the glaze: In a small bowl, whisk together the granulated sugar, lemon zest, and lemon juice. Gently poke the top of the bread numerous times with a small knife or skewer. Brush the lemon glaze over the top and sides of the bread, then repeat until all of the glaze is used.

9. Let the loaf cool completely while the glaze soaks in.

Highfalutin Bread Pudding

Virginia Living magazine asked me to come up with a bread pudding recipe just as I was trying to figure out what to do with some leftover loaves of Uncle Stan's Harvest Wheat bread (page 160) languishing in our freezer. It was fate. This extravagant-tasting yet simply made bread pudding, full of butter, cream, fruit, and nuts, makes for a hearty dessert perfect for crisp fall evenings. I like to ladle warmed Grand Champion Peach and Ginger Jam (page 186), Sour Cherry and Almond Jam (page 192), or Pear Butter (page 197) over the bread pudding just before serving. Whipped cream on top of it all is not out of the question.

1 tablespoon unsalted butter, at room temperature

2 cups heavy cream

2 cups whole milk

2 teaspoons pure vanilla extract

1½ cups granulated sugar

1 cup sorghum syrup or pure maple syrup

2 large eggs

3 large egg yolks

1 teaspoon kosher salt

1 teaspoon orange zest

½ teaspoon ground allspice

½ teaspoon ground cardamom

1 loaf Uncle Stan's Harvest Wheat (page 160, or use store-bought)

2 tablespoons turbinado sugar

Jam, warmed, and/or whipped cream, for serving (optional)

1. Preheat the oven to 350°F. Liberally coat the sides and bottom of a 2-quart casserole dish with the butter.

2. In a medium saucepan, combine the cream and milk and heat over low heat, stirring frequently, until just bubbling. Remove the pan from the heat. Whisk in the vanilla, granulated sugar, sorghum syrup, eggs, and egg yolks. Add the salt, orange zest, allspice, and cardamom. Remove the pan from the heat.

3. Evenly distribute the torn bread over the prepared dish. Pour the milk mixture over the bread. Using a wooden spoon, gently stir the bread to allow it to soak up the liquid. Sprinkle the turbinado sugar over the top. Bake for 30 to 45 minutes, until the pudding is puffy and golden brown.

4. Serve with warm jam or fruit butter and a dollop of whipped cream, if you like.

Skillet Cornbread
WITH PIMENTO CHEESE FROSTING

Makes one 10-inch cornbread

Here at the Red Truck, we've long dreamed of a cornbread filled with pimento cheese. We decided to put two of the spread's biggest personality traits—roasted red peppers and smoked paprika—in the cornbread itself, then topped it with a savory pimento cheese icing. As if that wasn't enough, we sprinkled on candied bacon bits sweetened with sorghum syrup and added a hit of black pepper. It'll terrify Southern cornbread purists, but this delicious beauty, baked in a sizzling cast-iron skillet, makes for a gorgeous presentation at the table.

BACON:

12 bacon slices

¼ cup sorghum syrup

¼ teaspoon freshly ground black pepper

CORNBREAD:

Nonstick cooking spray

2½ cups unbleached all-purpose flour, sifted

1 cup cornmeal

2 teaspoons baking powder

1 teaspoon baking soda

1 teaspoon smoked paprika

1 teaspoon kosher salt

½ cup sugar

15 tablespoons butter (1 stick plus 7 tablespoons), chilled and cubed

2 cups buttermilk, plus more for brushing

¼ cup diced jarred roasted red peppers

1½ teaspoons finely chopped fresh chives

2 teaspoons finely diced pickled jalapeños

1 cup fresh or thawed frozen corn

Sea salt and freshly ground black pepper

PIMENTO CHEESE FROSTING:

1 cup cream cheese

½ cup grated Cheddar cheese

¼ cup grated pepper Jack cheese

1 tablespoon buttermilk

2 teaspoons pickled jalapeño brine (from the jar)

1 teaspoon Rooster's Pepper Jelly (page 195, or use store-bought)

1 teaspoon honey

1 tablespoon diced jarred roasted red peppers

¼ teaspoon kosher salt

½ teaspoon smoked paprika

Cayenne pepper

1. Preheat the oven to 350°F.

2. Make the bacon: Place a raised wire rack inside a rimmed baking sheet. Arrange the bacon on the rack, spacing the slices apart, and bake for 7 minutes. Meanwhile, in a small bowl, combine the sorghum syrup and black pepper. Remove the bacon from the oven and brush the sorghum mixture on both sides of 4 slices of bacon. Return the pan to the oven and bake for 7 minutes more, until rich brown.

3. Let cool, then finely dice the sorghum-glazed bacon and set aside. Chop the regular bacon into ½-inch pieces and set aside separately. Leave the oven on.

4. Make the cornbread: Coat a 10-inch cast iron skillet with nonstick spray.

(recipe continues)

5. In the bowl of a stand mixer fitted with the paddle attachment, combine the flour, cornmeal, baking powder, baking soda, smoked paprika, kosher salt, and sugar. Beat on low speed to incorporate. Add the butter and beat on low speed until broken down into pea-sized pieces. Add the buttermilk, roasted red peppers, chives, plain bacon, jalapeños, and corn. Mix on medium speed to combine.

6. Pour the batter into the prepared skillet. Brush the top with buttermilk and sprinkle with sea salt and black pepper. Bake for 70 minutes, turning the skillet halfway through, until golden brown and a knife inserted into the center comes out clean. Let cool.

7. **Meanwhile, make the frosting:** In a food processor, combine the cream cheese, Cheddar, pepper Jack, buttermilk, jalapeño brine, pepper jelly, honey, roasted red peppers, kosher salt, smoked paprika, and cayenne to taste and process until smooth.

8. Spread the frosting evenly over the top of the cooled cornbread. Sprinkle with the sorghum-glazed bacon bits to finish.

Farmhouse Beer Bread

Makes two 8½ x 4½-inch loaves

Just outside Warrenton in Casanova, Powers Farm & Brewery owners Kevin and Melody Powers grow hops alongside a staggering array of heirloom fruits, vegetables, and botanicals, which they transform into an inventive variety of beers: think elderflower kolsch, blackberry saison, and lemongrass pilsner. I had been working on a beer bread for a long time, but the results weren't toast-worthy. When I ran into the Powers at a farm dinner, I asked for some ideas, and we discussed a recipe powered by their Belgian Blonde brew and studded with all sorts of Italian accents—Parmesan cheese, fresh herbs, and sun-dried tomatoes. After playing around with it and dialing up all the add-ins, we arrived at this hearty loaf.

If you're unable to find their Belgian Blonde beer, use any pale ale. Suitable substitutes found nationwide are Ommegang Cooperstown Ale, Allagash White, and Orval Trappist Ale.

Nonstick cooking spray
3 cups unbleached all-purpose flour, sifted
1 tablespoon baking powder
½ teaspoon kosher salt
¼ cup packed dark brown sugar
2 tablespoons chopped fresh rosemary
2 tablespoons chopped fresh chives
2 tablespoons chopped fresh basil
2 tablespoons chopped fresh thyme
4 garlic cloves, minced
12 dry-packed sun-dried tomatoes, diced
2 cups shredded Parmesan cheese
½ teaspoon freshly ground black pepper
1 (12-ounce) can blonde ale
4 tablespoons (½ stick) unsalted butter, melted

1. Preheat the oven to 375°F. Coat an 8½ x 4½-inch loaf pan with nonstick spray.

2. In a large bowl, whisk together the flour, baking powder, salt, and brown sugar. Mix in the rosemary, chives, basil, thyme, garlic, sun-dried tomatoes, Parmesan, pepper, and beer until fully incorporated.

3. Transfer the batter to the prepared loaf pan and pour the melted butter over the top. Bake for 55 to 65 minutes, until the top is golden brown and the bread starts pulling away from the sides of the pan. Let cool for 15 minutes in the pan, then flip onto a raised wire rack to cool completely.

MEET OUR PRODUCERS
Powers Farm & Brewery
PAGE 216

Sweet Potato Panettone

Makes one 8 x 4-inch panettone

I love what potatoes do to bread; they're like steroids for the yeast and produce an airy, high-rising loaf. A traditional panettone is my favorite holiday bread, and I got to thinking about using potatoes, just as pie baker Jan Pouzenc was next to me prepping sweet potatoes for some of her pies. I liked the idea of that orange root working well with citrus and raisins, and after stealing a few of her sweet potatoes, already cooked and mashed, here's the magnificent and colorful result. It rises high in a tall, round, paper panettone mold, available at novacartusa.com.

½ cup whole milk

½ cup mashed cooked sweet potato (about 1 medium sweet potato)

1 tablespoon active dry yeast

2 large eggs

1 large egg yolk

2½ cups bread flour, sifted, plus more for dusting

1 tablespoon sugar

1½ teaspoons kosher salt

¼ teaspoon ground cardamom

¼ teaspoon ground mace

¼ teaspoon ground or freshly grated nutmeg

4 tablespoons (½ stick) unsalted butter, at room temperature

1 teaspoon grated fresh ginger

1 tablespoon plus 1 teaspoon orange zest

2 tablespoons fresh orange juice

1 tablespoon sorghum syrup

1 tablespoon bourbon

1 cup candied orange peel (see page 201), cut into 1-inch matchsticks

2 cups dried cranberries

Nonstick cooking spray

1. In a medium saucepan, combine the milk and the mashed sweet potato and gently heat over low heat until just warm, not hot. Remove the pan from the heat, stir in the yeast, cover, and set aside for 30 minutes until foamy.

2. Transfer the yeast mixture to the bowl of a stand mixer fitted with the dough hook. With the mixer running on medium speed, add the eggs and egg yolk one at a time, mixing until just incorporated. Add ½ cup of the flour and mix on medium speed for 5 minutes. Add the sugar, salt, cardamom, mace, nutmeg, and 1 cup of the flour and mix on medium speed for 5 minutes. Scrape down the sides of the bowl after each addition. The dough will remain wet, goopy, and thin throughout the process; trust this and don't add additional flour.

3. Add the butter and mix well on medium speed. Add ½ cup of the flour and mix well. Add the remaining ½ cup flour and mix well. Scrape down the sides of the bowl after each addition. Add the ginger, orange zest, orange juice, sorghum syrup, and bourbon and mix on medium speed for 5 minutes. Add the candied orange peel and dried cranberries and mix for 5 minutes more.

4. Coat a large bowl with nonstick spray, form the dough into a ball (as best you can—it will be wet), and place it in the greased bowl. Cover with plastic wrap and let rise in a warm, draft-free place for 2 hours. Punch the dough down and let rise for 1 hour more.

5. Punch the dough down again. Turn the dough out onto a lightly floured surface, but don't add additional flour to the dough itself—it should remain wet. Cover with plastic wrap or a slightly damp dishtowel and let rest for 20 minutes.

6. Preheat the oven to 400°F. Coat a paper panettone mold with nonstick spray. Set a raised wire rack in a rimmed baking sheet.

7. Transfer the dough to the prepared mold. Coat a sheet of plastic wrap with nonstick spray and cover the dough directly. Let rise in a warm, draft-free place for 40 minutes or until the dough has risen to near the top (but not out) of the mold.

8. Remove the plastic and bake the panettone on the prepared baking sheet for 15 minutes. Reduce the oven temperature to 350°F and bake for 30 to 40 minutes more. Gently remove it from the oven and tap the bottom. A hollow sound indicates the panettone is fully baked; if not, return it to the oven. If the top is browning too quickly, lightly cover it with foil. Remove the panettone from the oven and let cool slightly on a raised wire rack, then remove it from the mold and let cool completely on the rack. Store in a plastic bag at room temperature for up to a week, or freeze for up to 6 months.

Snacks, Spreads, Pickles, and Preserves

GRAND CHAMPION
Peach and Ginger Jam

Makes six 1-pint jars

Before the Red Truck Bakery was anything more than a sweet dream, I entered this jam in the Arlington County Fair. Peaches were coming into season and a friend gave me a tub of crystallized ginger, so I combined the two with some spices and made up a batch. The resulting peach jam ended up winning me four awards, including first prize and the title of Grand Champion.

The jam is a bridge between seasons, starring summer's last burst and fall's favored flavors. The rich sweetness of the peaches finds a comforting complement in the spices—ginger, nutmeg, cinnamon, cloves, and allspice. Nothing tastes better on a biscuit, and sometimes I'll add fresh rosemary to create a more savory glaze for chicken and fish.

You can usually find powdered fruit pectin in the baking section of the grocery store or the canning section of the hardware store.

About 11 large peaches, pitted, peeled, chopped, and slightly mashed (8 cups)

¼ cup fresh lemon juice

7 tablespoons powdered fruit pectin

7 cups sugar

1 tablespoon finely chopped crystallized ginger

½ teaspoon grated fresh ginger

½ teaspoon ground or freshly grated nutmeg

½ teaspoon ground cinnamon

Pinch of ground cloves

Pinch of ground allspice

Zest of ½ lemon

1. Sterilize the jars, rings, and lids according to the manufacturer's directions. Set a raised wire rack on a dishtowel or layer of newspaper.

2. In a large saucepan, bring the peaches and lemon juice to a boil over medium heat. Add the pectin and return the mixture to a boil. Slowly add the sugar, stirring continuously until dissolved. While the jam is cooking, use a brush dipped in water to clean off any that bubbles up the sides and sticks to the pot. Stir in the crystallized ginger, fresh ginger, nutmeg, cinnamon, cloves, allspice and lemon zest and cook, stirring continuously, until well mixed, about 1 minute or until sugar is dissolved. Remove the pan from the heat and skim off and discard any foam.

3. Carefully pour the jam into the sterilized jars, leaving ½ inch of space at the top of the jars. Wipe the rims of the jars clean and seal tightly. Transfer the jars to a canning pot and add water to cover by 1 to 2 inches. Boil the jars for 10 minutes, sealing them according to the manufacturer's directions. Carefully remove the jars from the water and place on the wire rack. Let stand for several hours until cooled.

4. Unopened jars of jam will keep at room temperature for about 1 year; opened jars will stay fresh in the fridge, tightly covered, for up to 1 month.

Bluebarb Jam

Makes six 1-pint jars

As a kid, my mom gathered huckleberries from the tangles of brambles dotting the forests near her Pacific Grove, California, home. Her mother made a wonderful jam from the fruit, which Mom said is similar to wild blueberry jam. This recipe began as an homage to her sweet jam, but evolved into its own when I added rhubarb (my dad's favorite) and grated fresh ginger. There's a lot of tang and a light hand on the spices in this condiment. Put it on Rise and Shine Biscuits (page 24), use it on a Brie sandwich, or spoon it over a few scoops of vanilla ice cream.

8 cups ½-inch slices rhubarb (about 4 pounds)

5½ cups sugar

6 tablespoons powdered fruit pectin

5 cups fresh blueberries (about 1½ pounds), rinsed and stemmed

Zest and juice of 2 limes

1 tablespoon grated fresh ginger

1. Sterilize the jars, rings, and lids according to the manufacturer's directions. Set a raised wire rack on a dishtowel or layer of newspaper.

2. In a large bowl, combine the chopped rhubarb and sugar. Cover; let sit for 1 hour to let the rhubarb release its juices.

3. In a large pot, combine 3 cups water and the pectin. Add the rhubarb mixture, blueberries, lime zest, lime juice, and ginger. Bring to a steady rolling boil over high heat. While the jam is cooking, use a brush dipped in water to clean off any that bubbles up the sides and sticks to the pot. Stir continuously for exactly 1 minute; remove from the heat. Skim off and discard any foam.

4. Carefully pour the jam into the sterilized jars, leaving ½ inch of space at the top of the jars. Wipe the rims of the jars clean and seal tightly. Transfer the jars to a canning pot and add water to cover by 1 to 2 inches. Boil the jars for 10 minutes, sealing them according to the manufacturer's directions. Carefully remove the jars from the water and place them on the wire rack over the towel or newspaper. Let stand for several hours until cooled.

5. Unopened jars of jam will keep at room temperature for about 1 year; opened jars will stay fresh in the fridge, tightly covered, for up to 1 month.

Helen's Crabapple Jelly

Makes six 1-pint jars

On the West Coast, crabapples start coming into season in August. My mom's aunt Helen made a memorable crabapple jelly from fruit in her front yard, and I sure miss it. When I wanted to duplicate it for the bakery and searched for "crabapples," I finally realized that crabapple is a generic term for a small wild apple and not a specific variety. I had some growing on the farm and gathered more from my friend Carol Reed's Alexandria, Virginia, townhouse. Sometimes simple is best. This has just two ingredients: crabapples and sugar. It works well on a cracker with some goat cheese and a glass of Foggy Ridge hard apple cider, and holds its taste on toast or as a glaze for mild meats and fish.

16 cups crabapples (about 4 pounds), tops and bottoms chopped off

6 cups sugar; or as needed

1. Sterilize the jars, rings, and lids according to the manufacturer's directions. Set a raised wire rack on a dishtowel or layer of newspaper.

2. In a large pot, place the crabapples and add enough water to barely cover them. Bring to a boil over medium-high heat. Cover, reduce the heat to medium, and simmer for 20 minutes, until the apples are very soft. With a potato masher or wooden spoon, mash the fruit and simmer, covered, for 5 minutes more, until softened and broken up.

3. Pour the mixture into a colander or fine-mesh strainer (you may need to line a colander with cheesecloth if the holes are large) set over a large container. Let the juices drain. Stir and press the fruit with a wooden spoon to release as much juice as possible.

4. Rinse and dry the pot and fit it with a candy thermometer, if you have one. Pour the crabapple juice into a large measuring pitcher and note the amount. Pour the juice into the pot, adding ¾ cup sugar for every cup of juice. Bring to a boil over high heat and cook, stirring continuously and skimming off any foam, for 20 to 30 minutes, until the mixture reaches 210°F on a candy thermometer or a spoonful of jelly placed on a cold plate turns firm when placed in the freezer for 1 minute. While the jam is cooking, use a brush dipped in water to clean off any that bubbles up the sides and sticks to the pot.

5. Carefully pour the jelly into the sterilized jars, leaving ½ inch of space at the top of the jars. Wipe the rims of the jars clean and seal tightly. Transfer the jars to a canning pot and add water to cover by 1 to 2 inches. Boil the jars for 10 minutes, sealing them according to the manufacturer's directions. Carefully remove the jars from the water and place on the wire rack over the towel or newspaper. Let stand for several hours until cooled.

6. Unopened jars of jelly will keep at room temperature for about 1 year; opened jars will stay fresh in the fridge, tightly covered, for up to 1 month.

Ham Jam

Makes 4 to 5 cups

Bacon makes everything better—even ham. Originally, the only pork in our jam recipe was Virginia country ham, but something seemed to be missing, so we added in a good handful of our buddy Allan Benton's acclaimed smoked bacon. It really should be called Bacon Jam, but Ham Jam sounds better. No matter what you call it, the sweet, savory, salty spread works well on burgers, slathered on a warm biscuit, or topping a grilled cheese sandwich. Smoked bacon is available anywhere, but the best in the country—and what we use—is available at bentonscountryhams2.com.

5½ cups large-diced applewood-smoked bacon (about 1½ pounds)

1½ cups chopped country ham (about ½ pound)

3 cups diced yellow onion (about 3 medium)

2 garlic cloves, finely chopped

¾ cup bourbon

½ cup brewed coffee

½ cup cider vinegar

1 cup packed dark brown sugar

1 cup sorghum syrup

3 tablespoons pure maple syrup

½ cup whole-grain mustard

1. In a large skillet, cook the bacon over medium heat for 20 to 30 minutes, until a good amount of fat has rendered and the bacon is golden brown. Reduce the heat to medium-low and add the ham, onions, and garlic. Cook for 10 minutes, until the onions are translucent.

2. Increase the heat to medium and add the bourbon, coffee, vinegar, brown sugar, sorghum, maple syrup, and mustard. Bring to a simmer and cook, stirring occasionally, for 25 to 30 minutes, until the mixture is thickened and the liquid has reduced by about a third. Remove the pan from the heat. Let the jam cool, then transfer it to a food processor and pulse until finely chopped and spreadable.

3. The jam will keep, tightly covered, in the refrigerator for up to 1 month. Bring to room temperature and stir before using.

MEET OUR PRODUCERS
Benton's Smoky Mountain Country Hams
PAGE 216

RED TRUCK BAKERY COOKBOOK

Sour Cherry and Almond Jam

Makes 8 half-pint jars

Our farmhouse in Orlean is home to four Montmorency cherry trees, given to us as a housewarming present by our pals Mark White and Linda Kosovych. These are true sour pie cherries, and when we have a good crop and harvest them before the critters do, they make their way into the bakery's pies and jam. Adding a little almond extract emphasizes the fruit's flavor while taming the tartness a little. The jam really tastes like a generous wedge of cherry pie without the crust.

6 cups sour cherries, pitted and coarsely chopped
7 cups sugar
2 (6-ounce) packages liquid pectin
½ teaspoon pure almond extract

1. Sterilize the jars, rings, and lids according to the manufacturer's directions. Set a raised wire rack on a dishtowel or layer of newspaper.

2. In a large pot, combine the chopped cherries and sugar. Bring to a boil over medium heat, stirring continuously. While the jam is cooking, use a brush dipped in water to clean off any that bubbles up the sides and sticks to the pot. Add the pectin, stir well, and return to a rolling boil. Cook for exactly 1 minute to set the pectin, then remove the pot from the heat. Stir in the almond extract. Skim off and discard any foam.

3. Carefully pour the jam into the sterilized jars, leaving ½ inch of space at the top of the jars. Wipe the rims of the jars clean and seal tightly. Transfer the jars to a canning pot and add enough water to cover by 1 to 2 inches. Boil the jars for 10 minutes, sealing them according to the manufacturer's directions. Carefully remove the jars from the water and place on the wire rack set over the towel or newspaper. Let stand for several hours until cooled.

4. Unopened jars of jam will keep at room temperature for about 1 year; opened jars will stay fresh in the fridge, tightly covered, for up to 1 month.

Rooster's Pepper Jelly

Makes 8 cups or 8 half-pint jars

I have a feeling Rooster McConaughey always makes an impression. He certainly did when Dwight and I met him at a barbecue hosted by Robert Duvall, a longtime customer of the bakery. A guy with a sideways squint and an unlit stogie sticking out of his mouth strode up to Dwight and asked, "Who the hell are you?"

After introductions were made, we realized this guy was the star of the reality show *West Texas Investors Club*, as well as actor Matthew McConaughey's older brother. It turns out he has been eating our granola and muffins for years, courtesy of the Duvalls. When I perfected this cranked-up pepper jelly, I named it in his honor. Any guy who names his son "Miller Lyte" deserves a spicy salute.

This sticky spread is the perfect condiment for breakfast sandwiches, daubed on a biscuit straight out of the oven, or brushed on a pork roast or grilled chicken. A 50/50 mix of green and red hot peppers works best; jalapeño and serrano is my favorite combo.

2 cups finely chopped green bell peppers (about 2 medium)

2 cups finely chopped red bell peppers (about 2 medium)

1 cup finely chopped seeded fresh hot peppers (about 10)

3 cups cider vinegar

12 cups sugar

1 tablespoon red pepper flakes

2 (3-ounce) packages liquid pectin

1. In a large, tall-sided nonreactive pot, combine the green bell peppers, red bell peppers, hot peppers, vinegar, sugar, and red pepper flakes and bring to a rolling boil over high heat. Add the pectin and return to a rolling boil for exactly 2 minutes to blend and develop the flavors. While the jelly is cooking, use a brush dipped in water to clean off any that bubbles up the sides and sticks to the pot.

2. Remove the pot from the heat, let the mixture cool, and refrigerate overnight in a half-gallon jar or covered bowl to achieve a jelly consistency. The jelly will keep in the refrigerator for about 1 month.

3. If you'd like to save the jelly for future use, sterilize 8-ounce jars, rings, and lids according to the manufacturer's directions. Set a raised wire rack on a dishtowel or layer of newspaper. Carefully pour the jam into the sterilized jars, leaving ½ inch of space at the top of the jars. Wipe the rims of the jars clean and seal tightly. Transfer the jars to a canning pot and add water to cover by 1 to 2 inches. Boil the jars for 10 minutes, sealing them according to the manufacturer's directions. Carefully remove the jars from the water and place on the wire rack over the towel or newspaper. Let stand for several hours until cooled.

4. Unopened jars of jelly will keep at room temperature for about 1 year.

Rhubarb Chutney

Makes 12 cups or 12 half-pint jars

Blushing stalks of rhubarb are an ultimate early spring ingredient, and its tartness lifts up both sweet and savory recipes. This tangy chutney bridges both worlds. It's swell on hearty meat-and-cheese sandwiches, or simply on a cheese board next to a well-aged Cheddar. It's also a great holiday gift, reminding recipients that though winter may seem long, spring is never that far away.

¼ cup extra-virgin olive oil

2 cups finely chopped yellow onions (about 2 medium)

6 garlic cloves, finely chopped

3 tablespoons grated fresh ginger

1 teaspoon kosher salt

1¼ cups golden raisins

½ cup cider vinegar

1 cup fresh orange juice

1 tablespoon finely chopped crystallized ginger

2 cups packed dark brown sugar

½ teaspoon cardamom

1 cup honey

1 cup sorghum syrup

7 cups ¼-inch slices rhubarb (about 3½ pounds)

1. In a large saucepan, heat the olive oil over medium heat. When the oil shimmers, add the onions, garlic, ginger, and salt and cook, stirring, for 6 minutes, until the onions are translucent. Add the raisins, vinegar, and orange juice, increase the heat to high, and bring to a boil. Add the crystallized ginger, brown sugar, cardamom, honey, and sorghum syrup and stir until the sugar has dissolved, about 5 minutes.

2. Add half the rhubarb and bring the mixture to a boil over high heat. Reduce the heat to low and simmer for 20 to 22 minutes. Stir in the remaining rhubarb and return to a boil over high heat. Reduce the heat to low and cook for 5 minutes, until the second addition of rhubarb starts to soften. You want the mixture to be thick and chunky, not juicy or runny. Remove the pan from the heat and let cool.

3. The chutney will keep, tightly covered, in the refrigerator for up to 2 weeks.

4. If you'd like to save it for future use, sterilize jars, rings, and lids according to the manufacturer's directions. Set a raised wire rack on a dishtowel or layer of newspaper. Carefully pour the chutney into the sterilized jars, leaving ½ inch of space at the top of the jars. Wipe the rims of the jars clean and seal tightly. Transfer the jars to a canning pot and add water to cover by 1 to 2 inches. Boil the jars for 10 minutes, sealing them according to the manufacturer's directions. Carefully remove the jars from the water and place on the wire rack over the towel or newspaper. Let stand for several hours until cooled.

5. Unopened jars of chutney will keep at room temperature for about 1 year; opened jars will stay fresh in the fridge, tightly covered, for up to 2 weeks.

Pear Butter

Makes 10 half-pint jars

Despite the name, this recipe does not actually include butter. Think of it in the same category as applesauce or apple butter, but with a pure, sweet, sparkly flavor. I love it on a slice of Uncle Stan's Harvest Wheat bread (page 160), as an ingredient in pear muffins, spread on a croissant or dinner roll, or to mix up my PB&J routine.

Comice pears are best for this recipe, but Bartletts also work well. If you can't find pear juice, apple juice works in a pinch.

½ cup pear juice

6 tablespoons fresh lemon juice

About 8 pounds ripe pears, peeled, cored, and cut into 1-inch cubes (18 cups)

¼ teaspoon pure vanilla extract

3 cups sugar

1 teaspoon grated fresh ginger

¼ teaspoon ground cardamom

Pinch of kosher salt

1. Sterilize the jars, rings, and lids according to the manufacturer's directions. Set a raised wire rack on a dishtowel or layer of newspaper.

2. In a large pot, heat the pear juice and 3 tablespoons of the lemon juice over medium heat, stirring until well combined, about 1 minute. Add the chopped pears and bring to a boil over medium-high heat. Reduce the heat to low and simmer, stirring frequently with a wooden spoon to keep the pears from sticking to the pot, for 20 minutes, until the pears have softened and are starting to break down. Remove the pot from the heat and let the mixture cool. Working in batches, transfer the mixture to a food processor and puree.

3. Return the pureed mixture to the pot. Add the remaining 3 tablespoons lemon juice, the vanilla, sugar, ginger, cardamom, and salt. Bring to a boil over high heat, stirring continuously. Reduce the heat to low and simmer, stirring frequently, for 1 hour.

4. Carefully pour the jam into the sterilized jars, leaving ½ inch of space at the top of the jars. Wipe the rims of the jars clean and seal tightly. Transfer the jars to a canning pot and add water to cover by 1 to 2 inches. Boil the jars for 10 minutes, sealing them according to the manufacturer's directions. Carefully remove the jars from the water and place on the wire rack over the towel or newspapers. Let stand for several hours until cooled.

5. Unopened jars of jam will keep at room temperature for about 1 year; opened jars will stay fresh in the fridge, tightly covered, for up to 1 month.

AUNT DARLA'S
Smoky Pimento Cheese

Makes 5 cups

Growing up in California, I never met pimento cheese until I visited relatives in the South. We would swipe the bright orange spread on Wonder Bread and in the groove of a celery stick. When I headed back to the West Coast, it was pimento cheese I found myself craving the most.

I tweaked a family recipe and named it after my aunt Darla from Bristol, Tennessee. I've given the Southern spread a touch of her beloved Smoky Mountains by adding smoked paprika. There's a touch of zing in there, too, courtesy of some Quick-Pickled Onions. Sometimes I scoop this stuff right out of the plastic container with Ritz crackers, or, if I'm feeling fancy, I'll spread it on a biscuit and throw on a couple of slices of shaved Virginia country ham, or use it on a BLT.

½ cup jarred roasted red peppers, drained

½ cup cream cheese, at room temperature

¼ cup Quick-Pickled Onions (page 202), plus
    1 teaspoon pickling brine

¼ teaspoon cayenne pepper

1 teaspoon smoked paprika

½ teaspoon red pepper flakes

2 cups grated Cheddar cheese

1 cup grated pepper Jack cheese

1 teaspoon dried chives

½ cup mayonnaise

1. In a food processor, finely chop the roasted red peppers. Transfer to a fine-mesh strainer to drain off any liquid. Combine the cream cheese, pickled onions, pickling brine, cayenne, paprika, and red pepper flakes in the food processor (no need to wash the bowl first) and process until smooth.

2. In a large bowl, thoroughly combine the cream cheese mixture, roasted red peppers, Cheddar, pepper Jack, chives, and mayonnaise.

3. The pimento cheese will keep, tightly covered, in the refrigerator for up to 10 days.

Candied Citrus Peel

Makes 1 cup

These sweet strips with a bit of bite couldn't be easier to make. They go in our Old-World Almond Stollen (page 173) and Sweet Potato Panettone (page 182), but they also work well in cookies . . . or simply eaten on their own.

6 oranges or lemons, or a mixture of the two
1 cup sugar, plus more for tossing

1. Using a vegetable peeler, peel the citrus skin into long, ¼-inch-wide strips, keeping some of the white pith on. If desired, trim the peels to uniform widths.

2. Place the peels in a medium saucepan with 1 cup water and the sugar. Bring to a boil over high heat and and cook for 5 minutes, until the peels are soft and translucent. Set a raised wire rack over a rimmed baking sheet or some newspaper and, with a strainer or slotted spoon, transfer the peels from the liquid to the rack to drain.

3. Pour some sugar into a medium bowl. After draining, but while the peels are still wet, toss them in the sugar to coat. Let dry completely. Store in an airtight container at room temperature for up to 3 months.

Quick-Pickled Onions

Makes 6 cups

These red rings add zing to Aunt Darla's Smoky Pimento Cheese (page 198), but work equally well on a meat loaf sandwich (as we make at the bakery), mixed into potato salad, or piled atop a burger. Designed to be prepared fast and eaten soon thereafter, you shouldn't can them. These should keep for up to 1 month in the refrigerator, but you'll probably eat them all sooner than that.

If you don't have access to a ready-made pickling spice, you can make one with 1½ teaspoons each of mustard seeds, coriander, allspice, black peppercorns, caraway seeds, and crumbled dried bay leaf.

4½ cups cider vinegar

¾ cup sugar

3 tablespoons kosher salt

3 tablespoons pickling spice

6 cups thinly sliced red onions (about 3 large)

1. In a small saucepan, combine the vinegar, sugar, salt, and pickling spice and bring to a low boil over medium-high heat. Cook for 5 minutes to allow the flavors to infuse.

2. Place the onions in a large glass jar or heavy-duty plastic container. Strain the pickling mixture over the onions. Cover and chill for at least 3 hours before eating.

3. The pickled onions will keep, tightly covered, in the refrigerator for up to 1 month.

Jezebel Sauce

Makes 6 cups or 6 half-pint jars

Originating down on the Gulf Coast, this heritage sauce has long been a favorite of ours. Helen's Crabapple Jelly, peach preserves, and crushed pineapple play nicely with horseradish and whole-grain mustard to create an all-purpose condiment that's a little sweet with a subtle nudge of heat. You can whip it up in a pinch as an accompaniment for pork chops, spread it on sandwiches, or eat it on crackers with cream cheese.

1 tablespoon canola oil

1 medium yellow onion, chopped

2 garlic cloves, minced

1 teaspoon kosher salt

1 teaspoon freshly ground black pepper

2 teaspoons red pepper flakes

2 cups Grand Champion Peach and Ginger Jam (page 186, or use store-bought)

2 cups Helen's Crabapple Jelly (page 189, or use store-bought)

1 cup canned or fresh crushed pineapple

2 tablespoons whole-grain mustard

¼ cup jarred creamy horseradish, or 2 tablespoons grated fresh horseradish root

1 tablespoon sorghum syrup

1. In a medium saucepan, heat the canola oil over low heat. When the oil is shimmering, add the onion and garlic and season with the salt and black pepper. Cook, stirring, until the onion is translucent and starts to caramelize, about 10 minutes. Add the red pepper flakes, peach jam, crabapple jelly, pineapple, mustard, horseradish, and sorghum syrup and cook, stirring, for 2 minutes.

2. Transfer the mixture to a food processor and process until well combined and smooth. The sauce will keep, tightly covered, in the refrigerator for up to 2 weeks.

3. If you'd like to save it for future use, sterilize jars, rings, and lids according to the manufacturer's directions. Set a raised wire rack on a dishtowel or layer of newspaper. Carefully pour the sauce into the sterilized jars, leaving ½ inch of space at the top of the jars. Wipe the rims of the jars clean and seal tightly. Transfer the jars to a canning pot and add water to cover by 1 to 2 inches. Boil the jars for 10 minutes, sealing them according to the manufacturer's directions. Carefully remove the jars from the water and place on the wire rack over the towel or newspaper. Let stand for several hours until cooled.

4. Unopened jars of sauce will keep at room temperature for about 1 year.

Comeback Sauce

Makes 2½ cups

Technically a relative of remoulade, this classic condiment from the Deep South nonetheless reminds me of a slightly spicier version of In-N-Out Burger's secret sauce. Our version works just as well on a burger straight off the Weber Grill, as a dipping sauce for fried okra spears, or served with meat loaf or grilled chicken.

The prep time to satisfaction ratio is great here: since you just have to blend all the ingredients in a food processor, you can make this spread quickly for instant kudos.

1½ cups mayonnaise

2 tablespoons canola oil

¼ cup ketchup

1 tablespoon plus 1 teaspoon Worcestershire sauce

2 teaspoons Dijon mustard

1 teaspoon freshly ground black pepper

1 tablespoon hot sauce, such as Tabasco, or to taste

2 teaspoons sriracha sauce, or to taste

1 teaspoon smoked paprika

1 teaspoon cayenne pepper, or to taste

2 garlic cloves, coarsely chopped

1 cup coarsely chopped yellow onion (about 1 medium)

1. In a food processor, combine the mayonnaise, canola oil, ketchup, Worcestershire, mustard, black pepper, hot sauce, sriracha, paprika, cayenne, garlic, and onion and process until well combined and smooth.

2. The sauce will keep, tightly covered, in the refrigerator for up to 10 days.

Chicken Salad
with APPLES, GRAPES, WALNUTS, AND CURRY

Makes 10 cups (enough for about 10 sandwiches)

If I see chicken salad on a menu when I'm out for lunch, I'll always order it, but I'm really picky about how I like it. I want to see big chunks of chicken, red grape halves, chopped onion, and a pinch of curry. Unfortunately, it's usually a dry minced paste devoid of any flavor or texture on a slim slice of white bread—but I try it nevertheless. Luckily, I can always come back to the bakery and stand in line for one of our chicken sandwiches. We serve ours between springy slabs of Uncle Stan's Harvest Wheat bread (page 160) dressed up with a few Bibb lettuce leaves. And if beefsteak tomatoes are in season, throw some on.

2 teaspoons kosher salt

1 teaspoon freshly ground black pepper

1 sprig fresh rosemary

1 celery stalk, plus ¼ cup diced celery

3 pounds boneless, skinless chicken breasts

¾ cup mayonnaise

½ cup honey mustard

1 teaspoon curry powder

¼ cup diced yellow onion (about ¼ medium)

¼ cup diced Granny Smith apple (about ½ medium)

½ cup halved red grapes (about ¼ pound)

¼ cup golden raisins

¼ cup chopped walnuts

1. Fill a large pot with enough water so the chicken will be submerged when you add it. Add the salt, pepper, rosemary, and the whole celery stalk. Bring to a boil over high heat. Add the chicken and cook for 10 to 15 minutes, until cooked through and no longer pink inside. Drain the chicken, discarding the rosemary and celery solids, and let cool slightly. Chop the chicken into 1-inch pieces. You should have about 6 cups.

2. In a small bowl, combine the mayonnaise, mustard, and curry powder.

3. In a large bowl, combine the diced chicken, onion, diced celery, apple, grapes, raisins, and walnuts and stir to combine. Add the mayonnaise dressing to the chicken mixture and combine thoroughly.

4. The chicken salad will keep, tightly covered, in the refrigerator for up to 4 days.

GARDEN & GUN
Cheese Straws

Makes about 40 cheese straws

You'll always find the latest issue of *Garden & Gun* magazine at the bakery (and on the coffee table at my farmhouse). The magazine's editors uniquely celebrate Southern food, and I love their feature "Anatomy of a Classic," in which chefs put their spin on regional jewels. I was honored when they asked me to contribute a recipe for cheese straws. I dug out my grandmother's recipe, combined it with another recipe from my Tennessee cousin Roma, and added my own touches to create a winner for the article and what became a customer favorite at the bakeries. Ours are spiced up with red pepper flakes and three cheeses—yellow Cheddar, Gruyère, and Parmesan—and strewn with fresh rosemary and sea salt.

1 cup unbleached all-purpose flour, plus more for rolling

4 tablespoons (½ stick) unsalted butter, slightly softened

½ teaspoon kosher salt

1½ cups shredded sharp orange Cheddar cheese

¾ cup shredded Gruyère cheese

¾ cup shredded Parmesan cheese

⅛ teaspoon cayenne pepper

½ teaspoon red pepper flakes

1 large egg yolk

2 teaspoons half-and-half, plus more as needed

2 tablespoons chopped fresh rosemary

Sea salt

1. Preheat the oven to 350°F.

2. In a food processor, combine the flour, butter, kosher salt, Cheddar, Gruyère, Parmesan, cayenne, red pepper flakes, egg yolk, and half-and-half. Pulse until the dough becomes soft and starts to gather into a ball. If the dough is crumbly and dry, add 1 additional teaspoon of half-and-half; you don't want a wet dough.

3. Turn the dough out onto a floured surface and, with a floured rolling pin, roll it out into a roughly 11 x 8-inch rectangle about ¼ inch thick. Fold the dough in half crosswise and roll it out again. Repeat four more times.

4. With a spatula, carefully lift the dough onto an ungreased baking sheet. Trim all sides with a knife to create clean edges and cut the dough into vertical strips, a bit less than ½ inch wide. Cut each strip in half crosswise to make about 40 cheese straws. With the knife, gently separate the straws on the baking sheet. Sprinkle with chopped rosemary and sea salt.

5. Bake for 20 to 25 minutes, turning the baking sheet after 10 minutes, until golden. Let cool briefly on the pan, then transfer the cheese straws to a raised wire rack to cool completely. Store in an airtight container at room temperature for up to 1 week.

Okra Pickles

Makes eight 1-pint jars

Yep, I know—okra has a slimy reputation and is an acquired taste. I was one of the fearful. But Dwight, who grew up on North Carolina barbecue and Southern collards, knew the value of okra to complete a meal. I tried it and became a convert and, really, an okra cheerleader. We're quite taken with these spicy pickles, which complete a salad and partner nicely with chopped barbecue.

When choosing okra, look for young, tender pods without any bruising. They should be roughly the same size, about 4 inches long. Anything larger tends to be tough and fibrous, and you'll have a rough time jamming them into squat jars. And, if you have the chance, grow them yourself—the plant, flowers, and pods are showstoppers.

3 cups distilled white vinegar

½ cup plus 2 tablespoons pickling salt

2 teaspoons dill seeds

8 medium-large garlic cloves

8 small sprigs fresh dill

8 small fresh hot peppers, such as serranos, each about 4 inches long

3 pounds young okra pods, each about 4 inches long, stemmed

1. Sterilize the jars, rings, and lids according to the manufacturer's directions.

2. In a large nonreactive pan, combine 3 cups water, the vinegar, salt, and dill seeds. Bring to a boil over high heat.

3. Place 1 garlic clove, 1 small sprig of dill, and 1 hot pepper in each jar. Pack the okra tightly into the jars, alternating the direction of the pods (one pointed down, the next one pointed up). Divide the boiling pickling mixture among the jars, leaving about ½ inch of space at the top of each. (The dill seeds may have settled at the bottom of the pot, so use a spoon to get them out and distribute them evenly among the jars.)

4. Wipe the rims of the jars clean and seal tightly. The pickled okra will keep, tightly covered, in the refrigerator for up to 3 weeks. For the crispiest, most flavorful pickles, wait at least 1 week before opening a jar and crunching on them.

5. If you'd like to save the okra for future use, set a raised wire rack on a dishtowel or layer of newspaper. Transfer the jars to a canning pot and add water to cover by 1 to 2 inches. Boil the jars for 10 minutes, sealing them according to the manufacturer's directions. Carefully remove the jars from the water and place on the wire rack over the towel or newspaper. Let stand for several hours until cooled.

6. Unopened jars of okra pickles will keep at room temperature for about 1 year; opened jars will keep, tightly covered, in the refrigerator for up to 3 weeks.

Jack's Sweet Pickles

Makes six 1-pint jars

Dwight's father, Jack, was proud of these pickles. He had every right to be—I sure appreciated having him teach me how to make these. Crisp slices of cucumber bathe in a sugary syrup mixed with fresh ginger, turmeric, yellow mustard seeds, coriander seeds, and celery seeds.

It takes a few weeks to make these pickles, but the time and effort are worth it. For the first stage of the recipe, you will need a 3- or 5-gallon ceramic crock, which you can pick up at any hardware store or online.

Alum is a preserving agent that can usually be found in the baking section of the grocery store or the canning section of the hardware store.

1½ cups kosher salt

About 5 pounds pickling cucumbers, such as Kirby, sliced into ¼-inch-thick rounds (16 cups)

1 teaspoon alum

8 cups cider vinegar

2 tablespoons grated fresh ginger

2 tablespoons ground turmeric

2 tablespoons yellow mustard seeds

1 tablespoon coriander seeds

2 teaspoons celery seeds

2 cups sugar; or as needed

1. Day 1. In a large pot, combine 11 cups water and the kosher salt and bring to a boil. Put the sliced cucumbers in a 3- or 5-gallon ceramic crock, pour the brine over the cucumbers, cover, and leave at room temperature for 24 hours.

2. Day 2. Drain the cucumbers and return them to the rinsed-out crock. In a large pot, combine the alum and 2 quarts water and bring to a boil. Pour the boiling water over the cucumbers, cover, and leave at room temperature for 24 hours.

3. Day 3. Drain the cucumbers and return them to the crock. In a large pot, bring 2 quarts water to a boil. Pour the boiling water over the cucumbers, cover, and leave at room temperature for 24 hours.

4. Day 4. Drain the cucumbers and return them to the crock. In a large pot, combine the vinegar, ginger, turmeric, mustard seeds, coriander seeds, and celery seeds and bring to a boil. Reduce the heat and simmer for 20 minutes. Pour the vinegar mixture over the cucumbers, cover, and leave at room temperature for 10 days.

5. Day 14. Drain the cucumbers. Return half the cucumbers to the crock and cover with a ½-inch-thick layer of sugar, then top with the remaining cucumbers. Cover the crock and leave at room temperature for 7 days.

6. Day 21. Eat the pickles, store them in the fridge, or can them.

7. To can the pickles, sterilize the jars, rings, and lids according to the manufacturer's directions. Set a raised wire rack on a dishtowel or layer of newspaper. Pack the jars with the pickles and cover with the sugary syrup mixture from the crock, filling the jars up to ½ inch from the top. Wipe the rims of the jars clean and seal tightly. Transfer the jars to a canning pot and add water to cover by 1 to 2 inches. Boil the jars for 10 minutes, sealing them according to the manufacturer's directions. Carefully remove the jars from the water and place on the wire rack over the towel or newspapers. Let stand for several hours until cooled.

8. Unopened jars of pickles will keep at room temperature for about 1 year; opened jars will keep in the fridge, tightly covered, for up to 3 months.

Meet Our Producers

Compass Winds Sorghum

At the top of a rise in the road wending its way through the fields blanketing Mennonite-settled Dayton, Virginia, you'll find the Burkholder family farm, Compass Winds. Here Joseph, his wife, Margaret-Anne, and their three young children craft award-winning sorghum syrup—and help keep alive a centuries-old Southern tradition. "Traditional dying arts fascinate me," says Joseph. "I'm doing things now pretty much the same way they've always been done." After "shirt-pocket level" stalks of tall sorghum grass are harvested from the land surrounding the farmhouse, the sweet juice is extracted using a hand-operated antique press. It's then boiled down to create a golden nectar unlike any other sweetener out there. It's smooth and sugary with a slight grassy undertone, which lends it a profound earthiness. This complex flavor adds a touch of Virginia's terroir and a mellow depth to baked goods, like our Southern Shoofly Pie with Sorghum (page 52), and in our Sorghum-Glazed Pecan Pull-Aparts (page 169).

Mt. Defiance Cidery & Distillery

Focusing on mid-nineteenth-century-style libations, this boutique operation is nestled in the heart of Middleburg, Virginia. Founding partner Marc Chretien takes keen pleasure in crafting outstanding small-batch specialty spirits that are equally enjoyable sipped or as a part of a baking project, like the rich, rewarding amaretto hiding a pop of Ceylon cinnamon that goes into our Almond Cake (page 153), or their elegant apple brandy invigorating our mincemeat pie. "One of our goals is to revive old classics," he says. "We want to bring these amazing products back for a whole new generation to enjoy." To make this happen, Marc and his distiller are constantly poring over vintage cookbooks, old distiller journals, and yellowed newspaper clippings to discover and recover lost recipes. When they can, they take a field-to-bottle approach to their products, growing the heirloom apples for their ciders and maintaining a flourishing herb garden with Roman wormwood, lemon balm, mint, hyssop, and chamomile for their old-world absinthe—"It reconnects us to the land," says Marc.

Bourbon Barrel Foods

When he was working as a chef, Matt Jamie knew he didn't want to do it long-term, but he was passionate about food and wanted to stay in the industry. In 2006, he launched a soy sauce microbrewery in Louisville, Kentucky, aging the concoction in used bourbon barrels. After the soy sauce came smoked sugar, which we've been using at the bakery since it launched. By burning oak staves soaked with bourbon, Matt imparts a rich smoke and boozy boost to raw sugar—already full of nice earthy, caramel tones—which we use in our Southern Shoofly Pie with Sorghum (page 52) and Bob and Buddy's Mincemeat Pie with Apple Brandy (page 72).

The Farm at Sunnyside

Nestled along the border of Shenandoah National Park, just outside Little Washington in nearby Rappahannock County, this certified organic, solar-powered farm is the epitome of conscientious agriculture. "Our team blends sustainable practices with environmental protection," says Gardiner Lapham, who owns the farm with her husband, Nick. "We care about the watershed, the soil, and the pollinators." Highly diversified crops spread out over forty-five acres—from blackberry brambles and apple trees in one of the state's oldest orchards to Asian pears, which are an awesome addition to our Upside-Down Pear Gingerbread Cake (page 139). Stroll through the woods and you'll find highly prized pawpaws. A giant garden boasts more than twenty

A. Margaret-Anne Burkholder and kids at their Compass Winds farm in Dayton, Virginia, pressing sorghum.

B. Marc Chretien, proprietor (left), and Peter Ahlg, head distiller, of Mt. Defiance Cidery & Distillery in Middleburg, Virginia.

C. Matt Jamie of Bourbon Barrel Foods in Louisville, Kentucky.

D. Gardiner and Nick Lapham from the Farm at Sunnyside in Rappahannock County, Virginia.

E. Al Henry at Jumpin Run farm in Mount Jackson, Virginia.

F. Patsy Marks, owner of Belmont Peanuts in Capron, Virginia.

G. Chuck Miller, moonshiner, at his Belmont Farm Distillery in Culpeper, Virginia.

H. Kevin Powers at his Powers Farm & Brewery in Casanova, Virginia.

I. Allan Benton of Benton's Smoky Mountain Country Hams in Madisonville, Tennessee.

RED TRUCK BAKERY COOKBOOK

varieties of hot pepper, which give the right zing to Rooster's Pepper Jelly (page 195); pasture-raised hens fertilize the soil while feeding on discarded crops.

Jumpin Run

"We keep it simple," says Al Henry, fourth-generation owner of Jumpin Run, a thirty-three-acre farm just outside Mount Jackson, Virginia. Head up the dirt driveway to the fruit and vegetable stand he operates next to his home and you'll see signs for zukes, cukes, maters, and lopes (better known as zucchini, cucumbers, tomatoes, and cantaloupes). Lots of Al's stuff ends up in what we make—like Strawberry Rhubarb Pie (page 62) and our Green Tomato Pie with Bacon-Chedder Crust (page 100)—and we sell some of his produce at a mini farm stand of our own at the bakery in Marshall. Whenever Al or his son, Jon, walk through the door with flats full of heirloom tomatoes, bags of sweet corn, and crates of peaches, we get in line right behind our customers. The care he puts into his crops is evident in every bite.

Belmont Peanuts

The daughter of farmers, Patsy Marks married another farmer, and their family has been growing, roasting, and packing peanuts on its land in Capron, Virginia, since 1993. Planted on the first of May and harvested at the end of September, Belmont's Virginia peanuts are like no other variety out there—they're bigger, bolder, and crunchier. Cooked in canola oil, with some tumbled in a variety of spices, they're the best peanuts we've tasted. Each year we sell hundreds of their tins branded with the Red Truck Bakery logo, and we incorporate them into our Virginia Peanut Brittle with Sorghum (page 126) and Farmhand Cookies with Peanuts (page 115).

Belmont Farm Distillery

Chuck Miller is a scrappy moonshiner right out of central casting—white handlebar moustache, plaid shirt, weathered jeans held up by a tooled belt with a big silver buckle, and a Southern twang that doesn't stop. It's no surprise he's the star of Discovery's hit reality show *Moonshiners*. His hooch—the first *legally* produced in this country—is just as attention grabbing, which is why we use it to power our Double-Chocolate Moonshine Cake (page 135). Produced in the same style his grandfather used to illegally distill the fresh corn whiskey, it's a hands-on operation from start to finish. Stop by his distillery outside of Culpeper, Virginia, and you'll see the grain growing, the copper stills steaming, and a long line of workers bottling and labeling his spirits, which now have a worldwide following. It's a jug of Old Dominion history.

Powers Farm & Brewery

Husband-and-wife team Kevin and Melody Powers take an organic approach to farming obscure heirloom varietals. "We care what goes into the field and what comes out of it," says Kevin. Their abundant garden is fragrant with lemon balm and yarrow that grow among the tomatoes, yellow watermelon, and squash. Rising out of the fields are a rustic taproom and brewery forged from cedar cut down on the property. The enterprising couple brews seasonal recipes based on their harvest, including hop cones, herbs, fruit, and even vegetables. Their Belgian Blonde golden ale, made with their chamomile and ginger leaves, invigorates our Farmhouse Beer Bread (page 181).

Benton's Smoky Mountain Country Hams

I'm not sure which we love more: Benton's smoked bacon, or Allan and Sharon Benton themselves. For forty-five years, the family has been curing meat in the foothills of the Smoky Mountains in Madisonville, Tennessee, and the best chefs in the South haven't stopped lining up for it. We're all happy Allan left his position as a high school guidance counselor to take over a going-out-of-business ham company; he put it on the map with long hours, hard work and his grandparents' curing recipe. His bacon shines in our Ham Jam (page 191) and everything else that calls for this prized smoky work of art.

Acknowledgments

In a family of seven, I'm the oldest of four kids all with the same birthday (we're two sets of twins born exactly three years apart), so I've learned a thing or two about sharing—heck, I never had my *own* birthday cake until I moved out of state in my twenties. I'll be the first to admit that I need to share the credit of writing a book about my rural Virginia Piedmont bakery with the folks who helped me down this path.

Hearty thanks start with our recipe wrangler, Nevin Martell, an always-excited and upbeat food and culture writer based in Washington, DC. He first wrote about us for the *Washington Post*; that work grew into a friendship with a guy who keeps shaking my shoulders to remind me of what exactly the Red Truck Bakery has accomplished—something I've been too busy to see until forced to put it all down in writing. Nevin's enthusiasm took many of our good recipes to star status: who won't swoon over a Peach Milkshake Cake? Our mutual thanks go to his wife, Indira, and son, Zephyr, for letting him spend so much time in someone else's kitchen.

Nevin brought in our literary agent, Howard Yoon of the Ross Yoon Agency, and Howard's calm shepherding took this project painlessly from concept to an offer from Clarkson Potter to publication. Our mutual love for good whiskey and his wife's Ice Cream Jubilee sweetened the process.

Before I was a baker, I was an art director, and I worked with some of the best editors in the country. That, thankfully, continued on this book, with editor Amanda Englander at Clarkson Potter, who understood the Red Truck Bakery the minute she bit into our bourbon cake. ("A gift for Derby Week? Are you going to send us a cake for every holiday? I wouldn't be mad.") I've always been reluctant to turn my design projects over to another art director, but Stephanie Huntwork's award-winning portfolio quickly assured me that the book was in good hands and I could get back to making pimento cheese. Bringing food photographer Andrew Thomas Lee and his stylist, Angie Mosier, into the project was Stephanie's best decision; that duo's work is gloriously symphonic, and standing back and watching the shoot was so darned pleasing for me. Book designer Ian Dingman, who realized quickly that he and I were both type snobs, captured the feel of my bakery even better than I did. Thanks, too, to Danielle Daitch, Cathy Hennessy, Kevin Garcia, and Jana Branson on the Clarkson Potter team,

who reminded me of the most enjoyable parts of my publishing days. Additional appreciation was earned by our recipe testers; I hope it was delicious work.

Lots of advice bubbled up as soon as the project was launched. Ronni Lundy, the author of the double–James Beard–winner *Victuals*, told me to write about what I *don't* know: "Not *what* are grits, but *why* are grits. Dig deep and tell a story." Our loyal customers wanted to make sure their favorite recipes were part of the book, and an old-timer from The Plains, the next town over, offered up the legendary Mrs. Beavers's Caramel Cake hoping we could resurrect the decades-old recipe (I think we did well). Nevin and I took road trips through the Shenandoah Valley to chat with our tomato growers, peach farmers, and moonshine distillers on their turf. There's something humbling about standing in a Mennonite family's sorghum field a million miles from the city watching the children hand-crank the juicing press—it's easy to take for granted the backbreaking work behind the unique local products in our pantry.

My deepest gratitude and love, however, goes to Dwight McNeill, who introduced me to the South thirty-three years ago. He designed both of our bakery locations with only coffee and sandwiches as payment, kept me buoyed during the worst of times, and never lost faith in a guy who ditched a successful publishing career to sell his own baked goods out of an old red truck in the middle of nowhere.

• • •

Endless thanks to my earliest tutors, supporters, discoverers, writers, reviewers, artisans, and investors, including (in no real order) Mark Ramsdell, Connie O'Meara, Tommy Hilfiger, Marian Burros, Scott (Scooter) and Lynne Johnson, Carey Winfrey, Sandy Gilliam, Terri Lehman, Robert and Joanie Ballard, John and Beverly Sullivan, Jean Perin, Gardiner Lapham, Ken and Mary Thompson, Chuck and Dee Akre, Jim and Mai Abdo, Jonathan O'Connell, Alan Zuschlag, Nancy Raines, Mary Carroll Platt, Jon Meyer, Gurvir Dhindsa, Scott and Barbara Harris, Martha Toomey, Carter and Kathleen Nevill, Nancy Pollard, Darla Noyes, Molly Bland, Richard Moe, Faye Richardson, Eric Brace, Shawn Ireland, Daniel Johnston, Karen Wicker, Dot Long, Noel Mays, Franny Thomas, Ian Boden, Aaron Deal, Carla Hall and Matthew Lyons, Diane Flynt, John T. Edge, John Currence, Allan and Sharon Benton, Frank Stitt (who didn't mind that I stole his Highlands Grill lemon chess pie recipe), Claire Lamborne, Robert and Luciana Duvall, Jenny Marie and Rutger de Vink, Bill and Jeri Jackson, Jeremy Noel, Sheila Johnson and the Hon. William T. Newman Jr., Barry Dixon, Will Thomas, Jane Black, Jane and Michael Stern, Andrew Zimmern, Oprah Winfrey, George Stone, Lynn Nesmith, George Eatman, Allan Gurganus, Jennifer Maddox Sergent, Kathleen Penny, Haskell Harris, Erin Parkhurst, Francine Maroukian, Phyllis Richman, Tom Sietsema, Joe Yonan, Bonnie Benwick, David Hagedorn, Laura Hayes, Carol Joynt, Sherri Dalphonse, Ann Limpert, Lou and Ellen Emerson, Karen Hunsberger Adam, Kate Reynolds Ludwig, David DiBenedetto and all of the *Garden & Gun* staff who heartily embrace and celebrate small artisans, Vivian Howard, Justise Robbins, Adam Rapoport,

Carrie Morey, Jenée Libby, Matt Lee, Ronni Lundy, Elaine Chon-Baker, Claudine Pépin, Jacques Pépin, Jura Koncius, John McDonnell, Sally Quinn, Haden Polseno-Hensley and the Red Rooster Coffee team, Neal and Star Wavra, Doris Elam, Mary Putnam, Chris Ambrose and Laurie Fenton, Sandy Bieber and Linda Rosenzweig, Ben Cooper and Polly Gault, Abigail DeLashmutt, Jeff and Jamie Hedges, Mark Hyson, Scott Kasprowicz, Stephen Lofaro, Yak and Claire Lubowsky, Suzette Matthews, Mary Leigh McDaniel, Peter Schwartz and Anna Moser, Andy Martin, Rob and Stacia Stribling, Harry and Julie Bologna, Ryan Glendenning, Kristi Faull, Kevin Powers, Lauren Lee, Janis Golden, Caron Higashi, Jan Pouzenc, Judy Gutierrez, Liz Hottel, Lissa Muscatine and Brad Graham, Senator Tim Kaine, Governor and Mrs. Ralph Northam, Mary Chapin Carpenter, Cody Keenan, and Barack Obama: Y'all know why.

Index

Published in the United States by
Clarkson Potter/Publishers, an
imprint of the Crown Publishing
Group, a division of Penguin
Random House LLC, New York.
crownpublishing.com
clarksonpotter.com

CLARKSON POTTER is a
trademark and POTTER with
colophon is a registered trademark of
Penguin Random House LLC.

Library of Congress Cataloging-in-
Publication Data
Names: Noyes, Brian, (Baker),
author. | Martell, Nevin,
author. | Lee, Andrew
Thomas, photographer.

Title: Red Truck Bakery cookbook
: gold-standard recipes from
America's favorite rural bakery /
Brian Noyes with Nevin Martell ;
photographs by Andrew Thomas
Lee.
Description: First edition. | New
York : Clarkson Potter/Publishers,
[2018]
Identifiers: LCCN 2018002249 (print)
| LCCN 2018007069 (ebook) |
ISBN 9780804189620 (Ebook)
| ISBN 9780804189613 | ISBN
9780804189620 (eISBN)
Subjects: LCSH: Baking. | Desserts.
| Cupcakes. | Pies. | Red Truck
Bakery. | LCGFT: Cookbooks.
Classification: LCC TX765 (ebook)
| LCC TX765 .N69 2018 (print) |
DDC 641.7/1—dc23

LC record available at https://lccn.
loc.gov/2018002249

ISBN 978-0-8041-8961-3
Ebook ISBN 978-0-8041-8962-0

Printed in China

Book and cover design by
Ian Dingman
Cover photographs by
Andrew Thomas Lee

10 9 8 7 6 5 4 3 2 1

First Edition

"Whatever Brian Noyes bakes tastes so familiar and yet so surprising that I can never decide whether to tell all my friends, or hoard every bite for myself. Now I have another option: I can learn his tips and tricks and turn out my own crave-worthy treats. Skillet cornbread with pimento cheese frosting, here I come!"

—JOE YONAN,
FOOD EDITOR,
WASHINGTON POST

"If the Michelin Guide rated bakeries the way it rates restaurants, Red Truck would be at the top: 'Exceptional, worth a special journey.'"

—MARIAN BURROS,
FOOD COLUMNIST,
NEW YORK TIMES

"There are baking books for sightseers, who drool at the pictures and shelve the book with art. There are baking books for bakers—with recipes that sound so delicious you can nearly smell them on the page. *Red Truck Bakery Cookbook* is clearly both."

—PHYLLIS RICHMAN,
FORMER DINING CRITIC,
WASHINGTON POST

"Leave it to a baker who has past experience as a writer, editor, and designer to fashion a cookbook that roars on 8 cylinders!"

—MATT LEE AND TED LEE,
AUTHORS OF *THE LEE BROS. CHARLESTON KITCHEN*

"This beautiful cookbook celebrates what makes Red Truck Bakery a treasure for the community; it is a must-stop-by for travelers passing through. The next time you've got the chance, take some time to experience this place for yourself. You won't be sorry. And if you can't make it, this book is the next best thing."

—MARY CHAPIN CARPENTER,
SINGER AND SONGWRITER